The Con

A Poetic Cou
Communist l   ⸤sto

By Peter Raynard

Workers of the world unite! —
Karl Marx

First published 2018 by Culture Matters.
Culture Matters Co-operative Ltd. promotes a socialist and
progressive approach to art, culture and politics. We run a website
which publishes creative and critical material on politics and
culture; manage Bread and Roses arts awards; deliver cultural
education workshops to trade unionists; publish books;
and contribute to the development of culture policy in the
labour movement.
See www.culturematters.org.uk.
Feedback and comments are always very welcome, please email
info@culturematters.org.uk.
Cover image by Samuel Raynard
Layout and typesetting by Alan Morrison
Edited by Mike Quille
ISBN 978-1-912710-04-1

Acknowledgements

The author wishes to thank Karen McCarthy Woolf for introducing
him to the poetic form of coupling; Malika's Poetry Kitchen crew
for their support; and his family who have made various inputs to the
book, especially Samuel Raynard. The book is dedicated to the
author's parents, Peter and Gladys Raynard.

The author

Peter Raynard is the editor of *Proletarian Poetry: poems of working-class lives* (www.proletarianpoetry.com), which has featured more than 130 contemporary poets. His debut collection, *Precarious*, was published by Smokestack Books in April 2018. Peter is a member of the collective Malika's Poetry Kitchen, set up by the poet Malika Booker in 2001.

Introduction

In February 1848, Marx and Engels published the Communist Manifesto. It remains to this day a remarkable piece of literature, a lucid and powerful explanation of politics, economics and culture. It outlines the central importance of class in understanding human history, and a programme to guide our struggle for a more humane, communist society without class-based divisions.

One hundred years after its first publication, the German Communist poet and playwright Bertolt Brecht noted in his diary the plan to re-write this text in verse.

Brecht hoped to infuse the original text with 'new, armed authority'. The past century had witnessed ever-deeper crises and two horrendous wars. It had also seen for the first time in history a successful revolution in Russia, in which the proletariat had taken power. Armed with this historical perspective, the awareness of later Marxist theory, and the need to revive the idea of Communism as the only alternative to barbarism, Brecht resolved on this spectacularly ambitious challenge.

The resulting poem, 'The Manifesto', remained a fragment. For extracts from it, together with a commentary, see Jenny Farrell's article on **Culture Matters**, www.culturematters.org.uk

It is now 170 years since Marx and Engels published their masterpiece, and 200 years since Marx's birth. Neoliberal capitalism dominates politics, economics and culture across the globe, and brings with it incessant wars; avoidable famine, hunger, and homelessness; forced displacement of millions of economic refugees; and widening and obscene levels of inequality between rich and poor, and the powerful and the powerless; and the increasing corporate takeover and manipulation of culture—including not only the arts but sport, religion, and social media—which should liberate us and instead enslave us.

To mark the anniversaries, and protest these developments, Peter Raynard has written a poem with the same creative and critical purpose as Bertolt Brecht. It is a coupling, a poetic device which is a combination of an original text with a line by line poetic response. Applying the technique to the Communist Manifesto, Raynard brings out the prophetic relevance of that text, and its simple accessibility—and much, much more.

Because Marx never stopped being relevant, and accessibility isn't a question of language or ideas, but who has control of that language, those ideas; who decides what we read, how it's filtered, what it means. This poetic coupling is something else, particularly when combined with the vivid, jagged images that Raynard has sourced or created.

So **Culture Matters** is pleased and proud to present the poem, and we hope it inspires readers to revisit and re-read Marx's original, rethink their politics in its light, and, most of all, to follow Marx's dictum:

The philosophers have only interpreted the world in various ways; the point, however, is to change it.

Mike Quille
Editor
Culture Matters
May 2018

Contents

Dramatis Personae
(in order of appearance/reference)

John Maynard Keynes — The Pope — Donald Trump — Angela Merkel — Emmanuel Macron — Mikhail Bakunin — Prometheus — The Romans — a Big Mac — Chas and Dave — John Milton — the Naxalites — Dillinger — Ian Dury — Blur — Attila the Hun — Diogenes — Facebook — Super Mario — Pacman — Space Invaders — Alexander Graham Bell — UKIP — Kubla Khan — Chairman Mao — the Wurzels — Moore's Law — Iron Man — Aristotle — Harry Potter — Sean Spicer — Simon Cowell — John O'Sullivan —Grace Jones/The Smiths — Sleaford Mods — Captain Ahab — Woody Guthrie — Trades Union Congress — John Stuart Mill — Ned Ludd — Buzzfeed — the Chartists — John Fawcett — the M25 — Monty Python — Earl of Shaftesbury — King Oastler — John Fielden — Samuel Truett — Giuseppe Garibaldi — HG Wells — Franz Fanon — Antonio Gramsci — Quentin Reynolds — The Diggers — The Levellers — Gandhi — Nelson Mandela — The Suffragettes — William Rees Mogg — Joey Bada$$ — Gregory Isaacs — Rolling Stones — HP Lovecraft — Vikings — Rosa Luxemburg — the Chuckle Brothers — Tynchy Stryder — St Just — King Louis XVI — Pierre Joseph Proudhon — Bob Holman — Jeremy Corbyn — Joni Mitchell — John Cleese — Ronnie Barker — Ronnie Corbett — Fagin — Jimmy Carr — Bear Grylls — Isaac Newton — Jim Crow — the O'Jays — #metoo — Calliope — Clio — Erato — Euterpe — Melpomene — Terpischore — Polyhymnia — Thalia — Urania, — Sappho — Percy Bysshe Shelley — Coventry City Football Fans — Charles Dickens — Mary Oliver — Gordon Sumner — Adolf Hitler — Thomas Kuhn — Ken Dodd — TS Eliot — Lennon & McCartney — Bob Marley — Trigger — Roots Manuva — Eminem — Chubby Checker — Nostradamus — Benjamin Disraeli — Tom Waits — William Shakespeare — Tony Benn — Max Romeo — Dom Perignon — Adam Smith — The Clash — The Wicked Witch — Napoleon — The Bourbons — Johann Wolfgang von Goethe — Soul 2 Soul — Karl Gattungswesen — Friedrich

i

Nietzsche — the Scarecrow from Wizard of Oz — Robert (Rabbie) Burns — Frank Loesser — Groucho Marx — Thomas Coram — Octavia Hill — George Soros — Bill Gates — Winston Churchill — Emily Dickinson — Billy Joel — Gracchus — Reinhold Neibuhr — S Club 7 — Little Britain — Matthew — John Lyley — William Blake — Elon Musk — Spartacus — Georg Hegel — Fourier — Étienne Cabet — Friedrich Engels — Robert Owen — Sex Pistols — Farrow & Ball — Cannon & Ball — The Wild One — PF Sloan — Run the Jewels — Ant & Dec — Arundhati Roy — Paul Robeson

PREFACE

'Three-hour shifts or a fifteen-hour week may put off the problem
for a great while. For three hours a day is quite enough to satisfy
the old Adam in most of us!' (John Maynard Keynes, 1930)
he's having a larf,   in he? That's not what zero hours means

---

A spectre is haunting Europe
innit tho' what with Brexit, the refugee crisis, rise of the far right

— the spectre of communism
that red loose blanket in need of tucking in

All the powers of old Europe have entered into a holy alliance to
exorcise this spectre
*this unholy spectre come to remove the opium and Xanax from
the ennui of its existents*

Pope and Tsar, Metternich and Guizot, French Radicals and
German police-spies.
*Pope and President, Merkel, Macron, autoimmune free radicals of
capitalism, each with an I spy with my belittling eye*

Where is the party in opposition that has not been decried as
communistic by its opponents in power?
*our Karl saw a gap in the market before the market had been fully
formed*

Where is the opposition that has not hurled back the branding
reproach of communism
*no-one likes us, no-one likes us, no-one likes us, we don't care, we
are commies, dirty commies, we are commies from over there*

[1]

against the more advanced opposition parties, as well as against its reactionary adversaries?
we are coming with sickles and fists, hammers and molotovs, balaclavas and masks

Two things result from this fact:

I. Communism is already acknowledged by all European powers to be itself a power
albeit a power with a crackly track record of misuse, one dictatored with the ego of substance abuse

II. It is high time Communists should openly, in the face of the whole world
come out and tell it how it is FFS, it has been 170 years but it's never too late!

publish their views, their aims, their tendencies,
they tend to hang to the left, last I heard, but added ingredients can make it absurd

and meet this nursery tale of the Spectre of Communism with a manifesto of the party itself
ring a ring a roses you pocketful of posers, atishoo, atishoo, we will knock off your crown

To this end, Communists of various nationalities have assembled in London
to mark the 200th anniversary of Marx's birth, to honour his will, to update his worth

and sketched the following manifesto
give him a deadline and he'll give you a tract, the theory the practice, revolutionary acts

to be published in the English, French, German, Italian, Flemish and Danish languages
& Bakunin translated it into Russian, and we all know now how that turned out

Death is the veil which those who live call life;
They sleep, and it is lifted.

Percy Bysshe Shelley, *Prometheus Unbound*

A tragedy of the commons, of commoners, of plebeians, of all

Part One

Bourgeois and Proletarians

Part One: Bourgeois and Proletarians

The history of all hitherto existing society is
a Promethean tragedy in this late fading capitalist existence

the history of class struggles
for how else can society fail to deliver, the daily eating of a
founder's liver?

Freeman and slave, patrician and plebeian,
bounder and chained, leisured and leathered

lord and serf, guild-master and journeyman,
hunter and hunted, clubbable & refugee

in a word, oppressor and oppressed
indeed, indeed my trusty steed

stood in constant opposition to one another,
at the gates, the fences, the walls, the mind sets, whose serve is it?

carried on an uninterrupted, now hidden, now open fight,
across the fields of parliaments and palaces,

a fight that each time ended, either
by the courts, the jails, the coffins, the grave

in a revolutionary reconstitution of society at large,
where the muscle of power was clay, to mould the world their way

or in the common ruin of the contending classes
who now lacked the spit to lick their kin clean.

In the earlier epochs of history,
of which you may pick and choose at your whim

we find almost everywhere a complicated arrangement
such so it satisfied the fat palms of power

of society into various orders
though disorder of a nation lay bubbling below

a manifold gradation of social rank
a place for everybody, that didn't take place

In ancient Rome we have patricians, knights, plebeians, slaves;
with its neat plebiscite of division, a nostalgic object of derision

in the Middle Ages, feudal lords, vassals, guild-masters,
the thick rich cream with strawberries, anyone for tennis

journeymen, apprentices, serfs;
the barley the bread the pancakes the porridge

in almost all of these classes, again, subordinate gradations
for how else can society prevail towards its end?

The modern bourgeois society that has sprouted
leaving cold vegetables on a plate of privilege

from the ruins of feudal society
one of those gifts exported by the French

has not done away with class antagonisms
for they are the stuff of life, the dieters' dialectic

It has but established new classes
*from the super-rich to the precariat & moderately miserable in
between*

new conditions of oppression, new forms of struggle
call centres, welfare checks, PIP PIP, self-assessed deaths

in place of the old ones
so there are now two types of estate

Our epoch, the epoch of the bourgeoisie
the rule by the few to you and me

possesses, however, this distinct feature:
with the stink of distinction

it has simplified class antagonisms
which is very kind of them to do

Society as a whole is more and more splitting up
hot and cold, wet and dry, black and white dolly mixture failings

into two great hostile camps, into two great classes
quiet there at the back, and put away that crack.

directly facing each other — Bourgeoisie and Proletariat
Indeed, indeed, now pass me the weed

From the serfs of the Middle Ages
for which we have to thank the precocious Romans

sprang the chartered burghers of the earliest towns.
the quad stack Big Mac sheriff sweating over the little cheeses

From these burgesses
who were free from corvée and labour

the first elements of the bourgeoisie were developed
new town dwellers with economic means.

The discovery of America, the rounding of the Cape,
*those outposts of 'savagery' in need of civility, you want
developing? we've got the ability*

opened up fresh ground for the rising bourgeoisie
taming indigents with their own advanced type of savagery

The East-Indian and Chinese markets, the colonisation of
America
out of the blue blood veined erection of European ascendancy,

trade with the colonies,
where you give and we take

the increase in the means of exchange and in commodities
generally,
along with our viral intent, isn't that what you meant?

gave to commerce, to navigation, to industry,
those elements of stable prosperity, neigh

an impulse never before known,
which we fucking well know now

and thereby, to the revolutionary element
whose speed dropped a blast of death

in the tottering feudal society, a rapid development
Indeed, indeed, now pass me my steed

The feudal system of industry, in which industrial production
was a set of pipes excavated from the intestines of serfs

was monopolised by closed guilds, now no longer sufficed
because the human body parts were too emaciated

for the growing wants of the new markets
who were still yet to discover the delights of the flesh

The bourgeoisie has through its exploitation of the world market given a cosmopolitan character to production and consumption in every country

pat-a-cake, pat-a-cake, baker's man, bake me a cake much faster than you can.

Society as a whole is more and more splitting up

hot and cold, wet and dry, black & white dolly mixture failings

The manufacturing system took its place.
robots of various stomach sizes, blustered and bulged their way ahead

The guild-masters were pushed on one side by the manufacturing middle class
something the middle class did very passively aggressive like

division of labour between the different corporate guilds
confraternity contracts between belligerents, some say

vanished in the face of division of labour in each single workshop
atomising systems turning the metal of men into powder

Meantime the markets kept ever growing, the demand ever rising.
man-sized tissues no longer required, as it was nothing to be sneezed at

Even manufacture no longer sufficed
hands took to the machine not the article of craft

Thereupon, steam and machinery revolutionised industrial production
playthings of the mind, exponential change in fortunes, spin the wheel

The place of manufacture was taken by the giant, Modern Industry
all hail the shibboleths of mammon and their bloody tongues

the place of the industrial middle class by industrial millionaires
poor souls in the middle playing catch and missing

the leaders of the whole industrial armies, the modern bourgeois
come and have a go if you think you're hard enough

[12]

Modern industry has established the world market
connecting cracked palms that never shake hands

for which the discovery of America paved the way
with their independent isolationist do-what-I-say

This market has given an immense development to commerce
*so fly high my sweet nightingales of the east, you bulbul song
birds*

to navigation, to communication by land
enabling the troops of civilisation and Sodom to rape for progress

This development has, in its turn, reacted on the extension of
industry;
a cleaning up if you will of virulent middle-aged faces

and in proportion as industry, commerce, navigation, railways
extended
like a pop-up book with a mind of its own

in the same proportion the bourgeoisie developed
maturing like cancerous cheese on a wood-rot board

increased its capital, and pushed into the background
its nodules of self-aggrandisement, displacing

every class handed down from the Middle Ages
and so say some of us, and so say some of us, for

We see, therefore, how the modern bourgeoisie
the one percent to you and me

is itself the product of a long course of development
yes, yes, yes, we know what you meant

of a series of revolutions in the modes of production and of
exchange
round and round we go, where will we stop — hold on, I know!

Each step in the development of the bourgeoisie was
accompanied
by the 'gertcha' of Chas and Dave eulogising the end of days and

by a corresponding political advance of that class
*who still dance on this parliamentary isle to Milton's 'light
fantastick'*

An oppressed class under the sway of the feudal nobility
as it was, as it is, as it was always meant to be

an armed and self-governing association in the medieval
commune
oh for those lazy, crazy anarchistic days, sat around a smoky haze

here independent urban republic (as in Italy and Germany)
where townsmen gave purchase to their rights with moneyed fists

there taxable "third estate" of the monarchy (as in France)
the 98% of us scrapping over a share of bronze medal

afterwards, in the period of manufacturing proper
the threads of stratification began to untwine

serving either the semi-feudal or the absolute monarchy
the Naxalites of India can tell you a thing or two here

as a counterpoise against the nobility,
it always comes down to standing, back straight!

and, in fact, cornerstone of the great monarchies in general *whose spines were now curving to the submittal*

the bourgeoisie has at last, since the establishment of Modern Industry
with all its rising fallacies and clocking on palaces

and of the world market, conquered for itself, in the modern representative State
the porous borders of innovative disorder

exclusive political sway.
you turn if you want to, but the old lady of England, is not for turning

The executive of the modern state is but a committee
with their bingo numbers to hand & Saturday night covers band

for managing the common affairs of the whole bourgeoisie
so not the main party to make us all free

The bourgeoisie, historically, has played a most revolutionary part
through the bread of their circuses it became a fine art

The bourgeoisie, wherever it has got the upper hand
by scratching each other on the back of it

has put an end to all feudal, patriarchal, idyllic relations
and so say all of us, and so say all us, and so

It has pitilessly torn asunder the motley feudal ties
the basic fealty between vassal and lord

that bound man to his "natural superiors"
not forgetting the women and children hiding under their stairs

Capital's getting married in the morning, ding dong, the machines are going to chime. We'll make a whopper, so swing that heavy chopper, and get me to the bank on time.

and has left remaining no other nexus between man and man
than naked self-interest
the ermine gloves are off, hands in the air, and so are all his robes,
never never

than callous "cash payment"
as Timothy foresaw, so began the wandering away from faith

It has drowned the most heavenly ecstasies of religious fervour
though people still cling to the hymns, the ones that tell the hour

of chivalrous enthusiasm, of philistine sentimentalism
the inn of oxymoron is closed, everything must go

in the icy water of egotistical calculation. It has resolved
to take that which is no longer yours and dissolve

personal worth into exchange value
that's debt to me and you, a driver of progress

and in place of the numberless indefeasible chartered freedoms
like a two-week beano in Marbella, with girls running from the
fellas

has set up that single, unconscionable freedom
don't say it, don't say it, let me guess, I know this one

— Free Trade
ah yes, of course, off course, so where are we now?

In one word, for exploitation, veiled by religious and political
illusions
I'm here, I'm there, I'm everywhere, but you 'ent seen me, right

it has substituted naked, shameless, direct, brutal exploitation
ah yes, un-reparative progress, but who will clean up the mess

[17]

The bourgeoisie has stripped of its halo every occupation hitherto
honoured and looked up to with reverent awe
*besides that of talent shows, reality TV, and who lives in the house
next door?*

It has converted the physician, the lawyer, the priest, the poet, the
man of science, into its paid wage labourers
oh how the poets do scoff at such a paid assertion, sighing, 'if only'

The bourgeoisie has torn away from the family its sentimental veil
that one love bredrin, sistren, I&I, forward

and has reduced the family relation to a mere money relation
you still owe me that fiver son, you thievin' little scrote

The bourgeoisie has disclosed
in leaked documents from the dark web

how it came to pass that the brutal display of vigour in the Middle
Ages
another time between the wars with hyperinflation, rising Nazism

which reactionaries so much admire
for they stuffed their coffers with the sore throat of others, who

found its fitting complement in the most slothful indolence.
*get up you lazy corner shop capitalist, there is much work to be
done*

It has been the first to show what man's activity can bring about
*with shiny glass towers by babel and able, turn on the telly we've
now got cable*

It has accomplished wonders far surpassing Egyptian pyramids,
Roman aqueducts, and Gothic cathedrals;
steady on, it hadn't even got going back then, hold the thrill until

[18]

it has conducted expeditions that put in the shade all former
Exoduses of nations and crusades
yes, the bile of its oil oozes into the crevices of corruption, war,
across the UN floor

The bourgeoisie cannot exist without
shouting out about repetition and economies of scale, beat your
meat, repeat

constantly revolutionising the instruments of production
until virtually the pure essence of virtue is virtual, a con

and thereby the relations of production, and with them the
whole relations of society
is based upon algorithmic fornication limiting the need for
physical exertion

Conservation of the old modes of production in unaltered form
what was it all about? it was about everybody out!

was, on the contrary, the first condition of existence for all earlier
industrial classes.
a knife a fork, a bottle and a cork, that's the way we spell new
work, right on, out of sight man, right on (D)

Constant revolutionising of production, uninterrupted
disturbance of all social conditions,
because the wheels on the bus go round and round, round and
round, with

everlasting uncertainty and agitation distinguish the bourgeois
epoch from all earlier ones
and all those who were to follow into this atomised internet thing
we call time

All fixed, fast-frozen relations, with their train of ancient and venerable prejudices and opinions are swept away,
and its effects? whether the French revolution or protests of '68,
it's still too early to say

all new-formed ones become antiquated before they can ossify
there is no such thing as the self-preservation society, so fly

All that is solid melts into air, all that is holy is profaned,
arseholes, bastards, fucking cunts and pricks (ID)

and man is at last compelled to face with sober senses his real conditions of life, and his relations with his kind
all the people, so many people, and they all go hand in hand, hand in hand through their park life! (B)

The need of a constantly expanding market for its products chases the bourgeoisie over the entire surface of the globe
It wasn't just the Hun, in the viral run rabbit run of capital gain, xenophobe!

It must nestle everywhere, settle everywhere, establish connexions everywhere
now everything is free when you give away the 'do re mi' of your personality

The bourgeoisie has through its exploitation of the world market
patter cake, patter cake, baker's man, bake me a cake much faster than you can

given a cosmopolitan character to production and consumption in every country
when the question was put to Diogenes, what country he was from, he said I am a citizen of the world

To the great chagrin of Reactionists
who retort, if you are citizen of the world, you are a citizen of
nowhere

it has drawn from under the feet of industry the national ground
on which it stood.
the tectonics of economics, so shifting, so dismal, so
misunderstood

All old-established national industries have been destroyed or
are daily being destroyed.
the driven coarseness of British cloth, undersold the purity of
Indian cotton

They are dislodged by new industries, whose introduction
becomes a life and death question for all civilised nations
abide the hand that slaps the backs of machines and faces of
workers

by industries that no longer work up indigenous raw material,
but raw material drawn from the remotest zones;
the mud and the cud, the mines of metal, to the raw dollar an hour
scanning images for Facebook

industries whose products are consumed, not only at home, but
in every quarter of the globe
yum, yum, yum, yum, yum, Super Mario Packman Space Invaders
of the mind

In place of the old wants, satisfied by the production of the
country
spuds & pints, cider onions, vinegar and brown paper, gimme,
gimme, gimme the slave of your labour

we find new wants, requiring for their satisfaction the products of distant lands and climes
mushy peas to avocado, humus for the second house, where'd the mango?

In place of the old local and national seclusion and self-sufficiency
where every country was an island without shores, what is mine, is not yours

we have intercourse in every direction, universal inter-dependence of nations
the allotments of the world are ours, so take your pick and go make some carrot sticks

And as in material, so also in intellectual production
the universities of the world are ours, so you can shove your reliquaries up your arse

The intellectual creations of individual nations become common property
we've got an app for that, so we'll take this sample of hot black rap

National one-sidedness and narrow-mindedness become more and more impossible,
no matter how much you fight us, our God our greed are on our side

and from the numerous national and local literatures, there arises a world literature
of English my man, pidgin or not, you must translate your way out of poverty

The bourgeoisie, by the rapid improvement of all instruments of production, by the immensely facilitated means of communication,

saw AG Bell born this year, with the teachings of ancestors ringing
in his ears — such hearing and such speech, ever before beyond
our reach

draws all, even the most barbarian, nations into civilisation
try telling that to that UKIP mess with its bongo bongo land
bonkersness

The cheap prices of commodities are the heavy artillery with
which it batters down all Chinese walls
from Kubla Khan to Chairman Mao, the cycle of power is a
thousand years

with which it forces the barbarians' intensely obstinate hatred of
foreigners to capitulate
educate, agitate, organise the opportunities given by rising capital

It compels all nations, on pain of extinction, to adopt the
bourgeois mode of production;
whether slave, peasant or worker, all our fingernails are black
moons scratching the sky.

it compels them to introduce what it calls civilisation into their
midst,
one person's civilisation is another person's terrorism

i.e., to become bourgeois themselves. In one word, it creates a
world after its own image
mirror mirror on the wall, is control by the white man for
evermore?

The bourgeoisie has subjected the country to the rule of the
towns
round and round we go, the cycle of money has an upward flow

[23]

AG Bell was born this year, with the teachings of ancestors ringing in his ears — such hearing and such speech, ever before beyond our reach

It has created enormous cities, has greatly increased the urban population as compared with the rural,
the fields and the villages now live off the gruel of the cities

and has thus rescued a considerable part of the population from the idiocy of rural life.
I am a cider drinker, I drinks it all of the day, it soothes all my troubles away (TW)

Just as it has made the country dependent on the towns, so it has made barbarian and semi-barbarian countries dependent on the civilised ones
where languages begin to lose their tongue, customs lost to freedom of trade

nations of peasants on nations of bourgeois, the East on the West
but remember millennial tides, for they bring the blowback of storms

The bourgeoisie keeps more and more doing away with the scattered state of the population, of the means of production, and of property.
reduce, recycle, reuse, the waste not want not bags with bodies in them

It has agglomerated population, centralised the means of production, and has concentrated property in a few hands.
polity put the kettle on the state, stato, estado, état, bring them to the boil.

The necessary consequence of this was political centralisation
the western waistband expanded as it scoffed up stick-thin appetisers

Independent, or but loosely connected provinces, with separate
interests, laws, governments, and systems of taxation
the invisible hand that giveth, did first taketh away and,

became lumped together into one nation, with one government,
one code of laws, one national class-interest, one frontier, and
one customs-tariff
one iron fist with a glove that fists all, time to bend over, no pride
this time with one's fall

The bourgeoisie, during its rule of scarce one hundred years,
how time does fly, faster and faster to the speed of Moore's Law,
such exponential potential

has created more massive and more colossal productive forces
than have all preceding generations together.
I am Iron Man, I travel time for future mankind

Subjection of Nature's forces to man, machinery,
Fire is both hot and dry/ Air is both hot and wet/ Water is both
cold and wet./ Earth is both cold and dry (A)

application of chemistry to industry and agriculture, steam-
navigation, railways, electric telegraphs,
the playthings of the western world in the hands of new-born fools

clearing of whole continents for cultivation, canalisation of rivers,
whole populations conjured out of the ground
ask not what capitalism can do for you, but what capitalism can
do to you

what earlier century had even a presentiment that such
productive forces slumbered in the lap of social labour?
so rise you bats, mice, hedgehogs, reptiles, amphibians, open your
eyes in unvanquishable numbers

We see then: the means of production and of exchange, on whose foundation the bourgeoisie built itself up, were generated in feudal society.
PARK LIFE!

At a certain stage in the development of these means of production and of exchange
which unstitched the meat-greased medieval feast of blocked-up chainmail

the conditions under which feudal society produced and exchanged,
the con of kingdom from owndom, with the eigenstoum without the geistig

the feudal organisation of agriculture and manufacturing industry, in one word,
INDEED

the feudal relations of property became no longer compatible with the already developed productive forces; they became so many fetters.
the nation state begat diplomacy, the most opaque of languages

They had to be burst asunder; they were burst asunder.
so put your pedal to the metal, the apocalypse here we come

Into their place stepped free competition
step right up, the quality goes in before the name goes on

accompanied by a social and political constitution adapted in it, and the economic and political sway of the bourgeois class
the tusk towers rise likes cocks to the skies, such interplanetary craft

A similar movement is going on before our own eyes.
now you don't see it, blink and you'll miss it, now you do, boo!

Modern bourgeois society, with its relations of production, of exchange and of property, a society that has conjured up such gigantic means of production and of exchange,
PARK LIFE

is like the sorcerer who is no longer able to control the powers of the nether world whom he has called up by his spells.
you're a wizard Harry, but even this is beyond you.

For many a decade past the history of industry and commerce is but the history of the revolt
what's that you say Kant? 'the world has no beginning and no limits in space, but is infinite, in respect to both time and space'

of modern productive forces against modern conditions of production
double, double toil and trouble, gwan burn like fire, mek cauldron bubble

against the property relations that are the conditions for the existence of the bourgeois and of its rule.
Everything is inevitable, so sit back and watch your demise, your choice — 3D or VR or VD?

It is enough to mention the commercial crises that by their periodical return
from the Roman panic of AD 33, to the stock market crash of the Chinese

put the existence of the entire bourgeois society on its trial, each time more threateningly
with 28% of the workforce idle, debt lining their stomachs, the Greeks are left with their civilisation.

[28]

double, double toil and trouble, gwan burn like fire, mek cauldron bubble

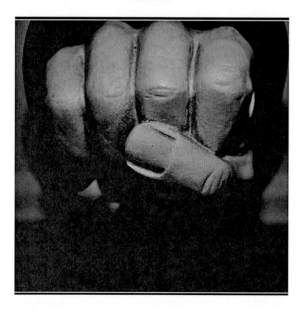

In these crises, a great part not only of the existing products, but also of the previously created productive forces, are periodically destroyed.
In the word of Sean Spicer, 'period!'

In these crises, there breaks out an epidemic that, in all earlier epochs, would have seemed an absurdity — the epidemic of over-production.
please sir, I want some more. WHAT? Please sir, I want....some more. MORE!!!

Society suddenly finds itself put back into a state of momentary barbarism
CATCH HIM, SNATCH HIM, HOLD HIM, SCOLD HIM

it appears as if a famine, a universal war of devastation, had cut off the supply
to live for a clichéd future full of silver white winters that melt into springs, for these are a few of my favourite things, the lifeblood

of every means of subsistence; industry and commerce seem to be destroyed; and why?
Please do tell

Because there is too much civilisation, too much means of subsistence, too much industry, too much commerce.
the too much too young bourgeoisie, have to push the boundaries, can't you see?

The productive forces at the disposal of society no longer tend to further the development of the conditions of bourgeois property;
fight the power, we've got to fight the powers that be, duh, duh duh,

by the conquest of new markets, and by the more
thorough exploitation of the old ones.
*Out of the ruins, we must sail East and South, round the Cape,
through the Canal, flushing the salt from the seas.*

on the contrary, they have become too powerful for these conditions, by which they are fettered,
ownership and control, man and tiger, key no lock, fear sick inside you

and so soon as they overcome these fetters, they bring disorder into the whole of bourgeois society, endanger the existence of bourgeois property.
Be careful what you wish for, lest it come true, untold riches for him and fuck all for you!

The conditions of bourgeois society are too narrow to comprise the wealth created by them.
the alleyways of the City, migrate east, forging great towers fed by driverless trains

And how does the bourgeoisie get over these crises?
Pray, do tell because we're still having to deal with their mess

On the one hand by enforced destruction of a mass of productive forces;
which explains the absence of flesh upon the bones of our feed

on the other, by the conquest of new markets, and by the more thorough exploitation of the old ones.
Out of the ruins, we must sail East and South, round the Cape, through the Canal, flushing the salt from the seas.

That is to say, by paving the way for more extensive and more destructive crises, and by diminishing the means whereby crises are prevented.
quod erat demonstrandum, a.k.a. you know it makes sense

The weapons with which the bourgeoisie felled feudalism to the ground are now turned against the bourgeoisie itself.
'this form of apoptosis is purely natural, nothing to worry about.'
'I never thought of hara-kiri like that before doc'

But not only has the bourgeoisie forged the weapons that bring death to itself;
When will its talents end? Get Simon Cowell on the phone.

it has also called into existence the men who are to wield those weapons — the modern working class — the proletarians.
To die — to sleep./ To sleep — perchance to dream:/ ay, there's the rubba dub dub, now who's got the soap?

In proportion as the bourgeoisie, i.e., capital, is developed, in the same proportion is the proletariat, the modern working class, developed
again, one begats the other, what is my disease is your disease, but only one of us has the vaccine

— a class of labourers, who live only so long as they find work, and who find work only so long as their labour increases capital.
idle hands walk to their local devil's workshop, beg forgiveness for the pleasuring by their palms.

These labourers, who must sell themselves piecemeal, are a commodity
come an' 'av a look, this strapping fella has fifteen kids and a front page tabloid headline to his name, who'll start the bidding?

like every other article of commerce, and are consequently exposed to all the vicissitudes of competition, to all the fluctuations of the market.
and nature is not happy about this great heating of its bath and all the steam that rises fogging the lungs and power's spectacles

Owing to the extensive use of machinery, and to the division of labour,
the zero hours left in a day, in an invisible contract, the what,
when, where, how

the work of the proletarians has lost all individual character, and, consequently, all charm for the workman.
no need for the three-year knowledge or educated lifelong debt —
need is but two arms, two legs and an empty head

He becomes an appendage of the machine, and it is only the most simple, most monotonous, and most easily acquired knack, that is required of him.
(ahem, for her as well remember), and even that knack is being
subsumed by machines — O inventors what have you done?

Hence, the cost of production of a workman is restricted, almost entirely, to the means of subsistence
open wide, feast your eyes, look what the food bank has inside

that he requires for maintenance, and for the propagation of his race.
but race as we know now, is a propagation of the bourgeoisie, to
dice and slice the poor you see

But the price of a commodity, and therefore also of labour, is equal to its cost of production
not anymore it's not, haven't you heard, the pied piper's coming
back to shoo the rats

In proportion, therefore, as the repulsiveness of the work increases, the wage decreases.
yo-heave-ho, yo-heave-ho, sing my sisters, yo-heave-ho, long way
to go, long way to go

Nay more, in proportion as the use of machinery and division of labour increases, in the same proportion the burden of toil also increases,
do you mean something like this?

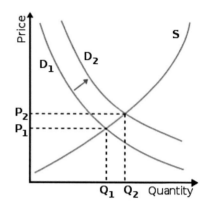

whether by prolongation of the working hours, by the increase of the work exacted in a given time or by increased speed of machinery, etc.
so here's the one that's driving me berserk, why do only fools and horses work? La, la, la, la, etc., La, la, la, la, etc. (JO'S)

Modern Industry has converted the little workshop of the patriarchal master
with his little glasses peering over his nose at the ship in the bottle, ahoy, land ahoy

into the great factory of the industrial capitalist. Masses of labourers, crowded into the factory, are organised like soldiers.
clocking in, piece work, sneaky roll up, stand by your lathes, attenshun!

As privates of the industrial army they are placed under the command of a perfect hierarchy of officers and sergeants.
your charge-hand, manager, director, owner, investor, hedge fund speculator, runner and riders, and they're off!

[35]

Not only are they slaves of the bourgeois class, and of the bourgeois State;
slaves to a rhythm they dance to, in their darkness, the hand in glove where the sun shines out of our behinds (GJ /TS)

they are daily and hourly enslaved by the machine, by the over-looker, and, above all, by the individual bourgeois manufacturer himself.
'we're going down like BHS, while the abled bodied vultures monitor and pick at us, we're going down and it's no stress, I lay and hope for the knuckle dragging exodus' (SM)

The more openly this despotism proclaims gain to be its end and aim,
the more they take apples from peoples' mouths, parade them without shame

the more petty, the more hateful and the more embittering it is
the horse withers, no longer holds the saddle, no longer hides the scars of utility

The less the skill and exertion of strength implied in manual labour
the more the muscles of men whither, atrophying brains, laying the ground to pass

in other words, the more modern industry becomes developed, the more is the labour of men superseded by that of women
from the playground, to the tills, to stacking shelves, paying bills, that Conservative lot blame the pill

Differences of age and sex have no longer any distinctive social validity for the working class.
we become mere psychological phenomena, test case sheep forbidden to bleat

All are instruments of labour, more or less expensive to use,
according to their age and sex
worker bees pollenating the pockets of private development, watch
our sting

No sooner is the exploitation of the labourer by the
manufacturer, so far, at an end, that he receives his wages in cash,
with no questions asked, the rich have enough to pay all of the tax.

than he is set upon by the other portions of the bourgeoisie, the
landlord, the shopkeeper, the pawnbroker, etc.
from one hand to another, empty palms to clenched fists, we
gather them to raise them

The lower strata of the middle class — the small tradespeople,
shopkeepers, and retired tradesmen generally, the
handicraftsmen and peasants,
a lumpen lot with ragged trousers, who can no longer afford a belt

— all these sink gradually into the proletariat, partly because
their diminutive capital does not suffice for the scale on which
Modern Industry is carried on,
money once floated around, like fish caught and put back in the
pond

and is swamped in the competition with the large capitalists,
whose nets have squares as small as an eye that cannot see

partly because their specialised skill is rendered worthless by
new methods of production.
economies of scale as a big as a whale, Ahab beware of the big
man's stare

Thus the proletariat is recruited from all classes of the population
the fight begins with the small fry first, the ones who suffer most
from the thirst

The proletariat goes through various stages of development
oxygen from water, protection from war, family/friendships, self-
respect, to be what a person can be

With its birth begins its struggle with the bourgeoisie. At first the
contest is carried on by individual labourers,
This land is your land, this land is my land/ From California, to the
New York Island (WG)

then by the workpeople of a factory, then by the operative of
one trade, in one locality, against the individual bourgeois who
directly exploits them.
in twenty so years comes the TUC, a combination JS Mill for one,
did not foresee

They direct their attacks not against the bourgeois conditions
of production, but against the instruments of production
themselves;
the Luddite fallacy is the long tail of economics that lashes up
against the walls of technology

they destroy imported wares that compete with their labour, they
smash to pieces machinery, they set factories ablaze,
Captain, General, King Ned Ludd, what stopped you from sticking
to the knitting?

they seek to restore by force the vanished status of the workman
of the Middle Ages.
don't look back in anger, I heard you say, at least not today (O)

compelled to set the whole proletariat in motion, and is
moreover yet,
for a time, able to do so.
*poetry in motion, see those hammers swing, such workers with
devotion, hear them poor boys sing*

At this stage, the labourers still form an incoherent mass scattered over the whole country, and broken up by their mutual competition.
at this stage, the monarch becomes otherwise disrobed, but is never in the altogether

If anywhere they unite to form more compact bodies,
squeezed tight as the mechanisms of a lathe, still told how they should behave, pass the swarfega there's protest to be made

this is not yet the consequence of their own active union, but of the union of the bourgeoisie
did they know of the impending overthrow, or were they too busy unwrapping their new lives?

which class, in order to attain its own political ends
it is always best to draw up a plan, when overseeing the felling of trees

is compelled to set the whole proletariat in motion, and is moreover yet, for a time, able to do so.
poetry in motion, see those hammers swing, such workers with devotion, hear them poor boys sing

At this stage, therefore, the proletarians do not fight their enemies
for they know not what they do, yet, so it is

but the enemies of their enemies, the remnants of absolute monarchy, the landowners, the non-industrial bourgeois, the petty bourgeois.
buzzfeed the following cultures amongst your workers, trust, flexibility, reliability, listen can you hear those algorithms whispering away?

Thus, the whole historical movement is concentrated in the hands of the bourgeoisie;
so invisible it's homeopathic, so flagrant it's nuclear

every victory so obtained is a victory for the bourgeoisie
and so say less of us

But with the development of industry, the proletariat not only increases in number
man can those boys breed, made to feed capitalism's need

it becomes concentrated in greater masses, its strength grows, and it feels that strength more
like you do in the second month of your gym membership, no?

The various interests and conditions of life within the ranks of the proletariat are more and more equalised
nice uniform, where'd you get that? Oh, it's the same as mine, well how about that

in proportion as machinery obliterates all distinctions of labour, and nearly everywhere reduces wages to the same low level.
what need is there for any pay gap analysis? When pay is a piss-stained floor that still shines

The growing competition among the bourgeois, and the resulting commercial crises, make the wages of the workers ever more fluctuating.
boom and bust, celibacy and lust, can anybody tell me if my pennies will rust

The increasing improvement of machinery, ever more rapidly developing,
from workshop of the world, to the world as a workshop

makes their livelihood more and more precarious
ah, 'you can't bring back time, like holding water in your hand' (JJ)

the collisions between individual workmen and individual
bourgeois take more and more the character of collisions between
two classes.
*it's take-to-your-corners' time: in the blue corner is Rich Uncle
Moneybags, with his portly moustache and shiny top hat*

Thereupon, the workers begin to form combinations (Trades'
Unions) against the bourgeois;
*& in the red corner, weighing in at 10 hours a day, six days a week,
one shilling an hour*

they club together in order to keep up the rate of wages
*'the principal force that transformed misery and despair into hope
and progress' (MLK)*

they found permanent associations in order to make provision
beforehand for these occasional revolts.
a percentage of very little can go a long way, keep plenty in reserve

Here and there, the contest breaks out into riots
*almost commonplace amongst the common, who wanted more
rights than a rise in wage*

Now and then the workers are victorious, but only for a time.
*pacified with morsels of reform, fed on scraps of freedom from the
top table*

The real fruit of their battles lies, not in the immediate result, but
in the ever-expanding union of the workers.
*spurred on by the Chartists, general strikes became more general,
solidarity people! That'll work.*

This union is helped on by the improved means of
communication that are created by modern industry
by this time, Isambard was in his prime, railway lines took
the news, turnpikes, canals across the land, not forgetting the
underground.

and that place the workers of different localities in contact with
one another.
combine, amalgamate, affiliate, bind, merge, unite, meld, mix,
bake for the next century or more

It was just this contact that was needed to centralise the
numerous local struggles, all of the same character, into one
national struggle between classes.
blessed be the ties that bind/ our hearts that fight for love/ the
fellowship of kindred minds/ is more than God above (JF) — yeah,
yeah, heard it all before

But every class struggle is a political struggle
for power is never a buy one get one free, do you shake a hand, or
shake a chain, or shake a money tree

And that union, to attain which the burghers of the Middle Ages,
with their miserable highways
was very much like the M25 today, stay in your lane, you're getting
in the way

required centuries, the modern proletarian, thanks to railways,
achieve in a few years
you may travel by steam, or so the folks say/ all the world over
upon the railway

This organisation of the proletarians into a class, and,
consequently into a political party
the nearest were the Whigs (don't laugh), who were a remote
country mile beyond a working class satnav

is continually being upset again by the competition between the
workers themselves
are you the Judean Peoples' Front?/ fuck off/ what?/ Judean
Peoples' Front? we're the Peoples' Front of Judea/ wankers!

But it ever rises up again, stronger, firmer, mightier.
with neither a sword nor a pen, but with a spade load of fight -
keep digging boys!

It compels legislative recognition of particular interests of the
workers
ah, now you've got parliament a thinking, the vein-nosed bastards
are slightly shrinking

by taking advantage of the divisions among the bourgeoisie itself
Ashley of Shaftesbury, the Factory King Oastler, the radical John
Fielden, saw a gap in the fence

Thus, the ten-hours' bill in England was carried
so children and women could see daylight, smell fresh polluted air,
outside the mills again

Altogether collisions between the classes of the old society
furthered, in many ways, the course of development of the
proletariat
Rome was not exactly burning, but neither were the working class
fiddling

The bourgeoisie finds itself involved in a constant battle.
even without war, there are spoils which cannot be ignored

At first with the aristocracy; later on, with those portions of the
bourgeoisie itself,
Trickle down ergonomics? Me thinks not, for musical chairs dance
to different tunes.

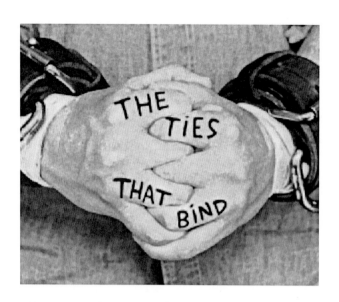

But every class struggle is a political struggle
for power is never a buy one get one free,
do you shake a hand, or shake a chain, or shake a money tree

whose interests have become antagonistic to the progress of
industry; at all time with the bourgeoisie of foreign countries.
this type of progress is a viral, a meme, cutting up cultures, faiths,
- you think they're in control?

In all these battles, it sees itself compelled to appeal to the
proletariat, to ask for help, and thus, to drag it into the political
arena.
and thus, dulce et decorum est pro patria mori, although where
that is, no longer applies

The bourgeoisie itself, therefore, supplies the proletariat with its
own elements of political and general education
A new empire desired to tame the wild borderlands for its own ends
(ST)

in other words, it furnishes the proletariat with weapons for
fighting the bourgeoisie
for who could resist, the offer of 'hunger, thirst, forced marches,
battle, and death (GG)'?

Further, as we have already seen, entire sections of the ruling class
are, by the advance of industry, precipitated into the proletariat,
come one, come all, some have higher places than others to fall

or are at least threatened in their conditions of existence.
Rub a dub dub, three fools in a tub, and who do you think they
be? The butcher, the baker, the candlestick maker, turn them out,
knaves all three

These also supply the proletariat with fresh elements of
enlightenment and progress
for until now there has been but the sigh of an oppressed culture
arising from the armpits of pulpits

Finally, in times when the class struggle nears the decisive hour,
as the bread goes stale and mouldy, and circuses are out of
fashion

the progress of dissolution going on within the ruling class, in
fact within the whole range of old society,
says it's time to embrace chaos as 'the present determines the
future, but the approximate present does not approximately
determine the future,' it...

assumes such a violent, glaring character, that a small section of
the ruling class cuts itself adrift,
goodbye dear wealth, I loved thee well, maybe too well

and joins the revolutionary class, the class that holds the future
in its hands.
all hands on deck, there is plenty of room on this sinking ship

Just as, therefore, at an earlier period, a section of the nobility
went over to the bourgeoisie,
they really had no choice you see, a different downward mobility

so now a portion of the bourgeoisie goes over to the proletariat,
and in particular, a portion of the bourgeois ideologists,
it was not their fists that were required, but the knowledge from
books they'd been denied

who have raised themselves to the level of comprehending
theoretically the historical movement as a whole
'there is no intelligence, where there is no change, and no need for
change', so what are you: Eloi or Morlock? (HGW)

Of all the classes that stand face to face with the bourgeoisie
today, the proletariat alone is a really revolutionary class.
'When we revolt it's not for a particular culture. We revolt simply
because, for many reasons, we can no longer breathe' (FF)

[47]

The other classes decay and finally disappear in the face of
Modern Industry; the proletariat is its special and essential
product.
*come one, come all, gather round my stall, for there is much work
to be undone*

The lower middle class, the small manufacturer, the shopkeeper,
the artisan, the peasant,
*whose existence was a flickering flame of a melted candle, became
a one and for*

all these fight against the bourgeoisie, to save from extinction
their existence as fractions of the middle class.
*you cannot beat someone into existence, blood flows in but one
direction*

They are therefore not revolutionary, but conservative. Nay more,
they are reactionary, for they try to roll back the wheel of history.
*'the crisis consists precisely in the fact that the old is dying and the
new cannot be born; in this interregnum a great variety of morbid
symptoms appear.' (AG)*

If by chance, they are revolutionary, they are only so in view of
their impending transfer into the proletariat;
*if you can't beat them (to death), join them, for the wounded don't
cry (QR)*

they thus defend not their present, but their future interests, they
desert their own standpoint to place themselves at that of the
proletariat.
*you've got to pick a pocket or two boys, you've got to pick a pocket
or two*

The "dangerous class", [lumpenproletariat] the social scum, that passively rotting mass thrown off by the lowest layers of the old society,
steady on, this suit is clean on, Sunday's best, they'll be no rat catching on this day of rest.

may, here and there, be swept into the movement by a proletarian revolution
there is much sweeping to be done, until we form a Vanguard and become all for one

its conditions of life, however, prepare it far more for the part of a bribed tool of reactionary intrigue
does this less than 'precariat' class lack the luxury of refusal?

In the conditions of the proletariat, those of old society at large are already virtually swamped.
just to be clear, this is a premonition - not yet a reality, it is just a welcome fear

The proletarian is without property; his relation to his wife and children has no longer anything in common with the bourgeois family relations;
any chance of the sex tonight love? Reproduction or pleasure? Er, pleasure? Ooh, come here you sexy bourgeois bastard!

modern industry labour, modern subjection to capital, the same in England as in France, in America as in Germany, has stripped him of every trace of national character.
yet stereotypes remain, just ask any stand-up comedian of old

Law, morality, religion, are to him so many bourgeois prejudices, behind which lurk in ambush just as many bourgeois interests
coming ready or not, we seek him here, we seek him there

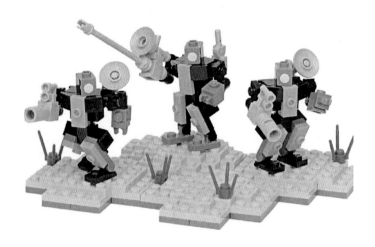

The proletariat, the lowest stratum of our present society, cannot stir, cannot raise itself up, without the whole super-incumbent strata of official society being sprung into the air
come on let's all fly in our beautiful balloons, we can fill the sky with falling failed tycoons

All the preceding classes that got the upper hand sought to
fortify their already acquired status by subjecting society at large
to their conditions of appropriation.
and you can't exactly fortify something that is nothing — nought
plus nought still equals nowt

The proletarians cannot become masters of the productive forces
of society, except by abolishing their own previous mode of
appropriation
which be the doffing of the cap, and mucking of the hands

and thereby also every other previous mode of appropriation
that'll be the thieving and gambling, womanising and fighting,
at least that's what the tabloids say

They have nothing of their own to secure and to fortify
for you may be prisoners, but there is no dilemma

their mission is to destroy all previous securities for, and
insurances of, individual property
and don't be giving us any of your French, La propriété, c'est le vol!
— Karl thinks it's self-refuting

All previous historical movements were movements of
minorities, or in the interest of minorities
shall we ask the Diggers & Levellers, ask Gandhi and the 400
million Indians in 1947, ask Nelson Mandela, ask the Suffragettes,
ask ourselves, is that not now in our past?

The proletarian movement is the self-conscious, independent
movement of the immense majority, in the interest of the
immense majority.
Now you're sucking diesel. Yes, let's give it to the Rees Moggs and
all those weasels.

Though not in substance, yet in form, the struggle of the proletariat with the bourgeoisie is at first a national struggle.
If you 'bout this revolution, please stand up/ We ain't got no one to trust/ Time is running up, feel the burn in my gut/ And if you got the guts, scream, "Fuck Donald Trump" (JB$$)

The proletariat of each country must, of course, first of all settle matters with its own bourgeoisie
with dirty dollars, come brains on collars (JB$$)

In depicting the most general phases of the development of the proletariat, we traced the more or less veiled civil war, raging within existing society
spread that map out like an open chest, trace the scars to the ocean of change

up to the point where that war breaks out into open revolution
just make sure you televise that motherfucker this time round

and where the violent overthrow of the bourgeoisie lays the foundation for the sway of the proletariat
and that is something we need to hold onto, but before that, let's start summing up

Hitherto, every form of society has been based, as we have already seen, on the antagonism of oppressing and oppressed classes
it's gone well beyond that mate, well beyond the pay me more, well beyond I can't buy that house, well beyond, 'you've got my vote', yes sir

But in order to oppress a class, certain conditions must be assured to it under which it can, at least, continue its slavish existence
Here beginneth the lesson again, but you can never learn too much.

The serf, in the period of serfdom, raised himself to membership in the commune
fucking hippies

just as the petty bourgeois, under the yoke of the feudal absolutism, managed to develop into a bourgeois.
fucking yuppies

The modern labourer, on the contrary, instead of rising with the process of industry, sinks deeper and deeper below the conditions of existence of his own class.
fucking chavs

He becomes a pauper, and pauperism develops more rapidly than population and wealth
'I'm only able to romance you, & make you tingle with delight, financially, I'm a pauper, but when it comes to lovin I'm alright. alright alright' (GI)

And here it becomes evident, that the bourgeoisie is unfit any longer to be the ruling class in society
I hereby declare the social contract null and void

and to impose its conditions of existence upon society as an over-riding law
reparations will be in order, palaces sacked, parliament will become a homeless shelter for the wealthy

It is unfit to rule because it is incompetent to assure an existence to its slave within his slavery
ask the Trade Winds which way they blow, from the West Coast of Africa, to the Caribbean shores, snaking the US east coast, swooping a loop to Cardiff, Liverpool, Bristol, beyond

because it cannot help letting him sink into such a state
like those who live in sink estates, dramatized by middle class
kitchen sinks

that it has to feed him, instead of being fed by him
soup kitchens of the world, can we not have a slice of daily bread

Society can no longer live under this bourgeoisie, in other words,
its existence is no longer compatible with society
Be gone, before I get my dad on you

The essential conditions for the existence
Lord, please gimme shelter, or else I'm going to fade away

and for the sway of the bourgeois class is the formation and
augmentation of capital
be it fixed, circular, or done up like a Christmas tree, they want it

the condition for capital is wage-labour
a deal breaker, no brainer, no need to lay your bets, everyone's a
winner, step right up

Wage-labour rests exclusively on competition between the
labourers.
who will buy my wonderful muscles, hands like shovels, the best on
the site

The advance of industry, whose involuntary promoter is the
bourgeoisie
'from even the greatest of horrors, irony is seldom absent' (HPL)

replaces the isolation of the labourers, due to competition, by the
revolutionary combination, due to association
thanks boss for the opportunity to overthrow the state, we won't
forget you

[54]

The development of Modern Industry, therefore, cuts from under its feet the very foundation on which the bourgeoisie produces and appropriates products
12th century nuns disfigured themselves to protect their chastity and were burned by the horrified Vikings

What the bourgeoisie therefore produces, above all, are its own grave-diggers
and with hands like shovels we are more than ready to bury you all

Its fall and the victory of the proletariat are equally inevitable
It's been a long, a long time coming, But I know a change gonna come, oh yes it is.

Part Two

Proletarians and Communists

Part Two: Proletarians and Communists

Freedom is the freedom of the dissenter; it does not rest,
not in peace, but within the, 'I was, I am, I will be!'
(Rosa Luxemburg)

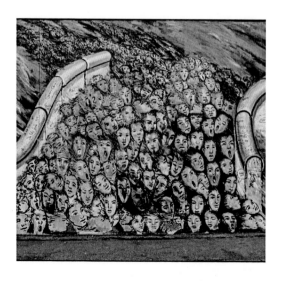

In what relation do the Communists stand to the proletarians as a whole?
dear ladles and jelly spoons the floor is now open for busyness,
who would like to start? Oh, sorry, wait, Karl has a thing or two to
say first...

The Communists do not form a separate party opposed to the other working-class parties
for they are 'the' working class party, and they are gonna bring it

They have no interests separate and apart from those of the proletariat as a whole
there are only two interests, those of human beings, and those of the bourgeoisie, see

They do not set up any sectarian principles of their own, by which to shape and mould the proletarian movement
Much of the backroom work had been done, sentimental primitive communism was to bow to science and be gone

The Communists are distinguished from the other working-class parties by this only:
now keep in mind the Chartists here, for Marx always gave them his undivided ear

1. In the national struggles of the proletarians of the different countries, they point out and bring to the front the common interests of the entire proletariat, independently of all nationality.
revolution within countries, across countries, without countries

2. In the various stages of development which the struggle of the working class against the bourgeoisie has to pass through
they were the rising bilge, set to keel the bourgeoisie into the sea, you see

they always and everywhere represent the interests of the
movement as a whole
they become the tides of the ocean, ever returning to dissolve
archaic power

The Communists, therefore, are on the one hand, practically, the
most advanced and resolute section of the working-class parties
of every country, that section which pushes forward all others;
Freedom is the freedom of the dissenter; it does not rest, not in
peace, but within the, 'I was, I am, I will be!'(RL)

on the other hand, theoretically, they have over the great mass of
the proletariat the advantage of clearly understanding the line of
march,
we was too poor to learn you see, not from books at least,
darkness was our teacher

the conditions, and the ultimate general results of the proletarian
movement
looking back from time immemorial we're still looking for the
right mob for the job

The immediate aim of the Communists is the same as that of all
other proletarian parties
there's nothing quite like the present, and 1848 was nothing like
the present, however

formation of the proletariat into a class, overthrow of the
bourgeois supremacy, conquest of political power by the
proletariat
looking back or forth, that sounds like a no brainer to me, a case
of Malcolm X's by any means necessary

The theoretical conclusions of the Communists
was it the French that said: 'That is all well and good in practice,
but where is the theory?'

[61]

are in no way based on ideas or principles that have been invented, or discovered, by this or that would-be universal reformer
non, non, non, we will have none of this or that type of revolution or party, c'est tout le monde!

They merely express, in general terms, actual relations springing from an existing class struggle, from a historical movement going on under our very eyes.
it's gone on forever, like the Chuckle Brothers' say, 'to me, to you, to me, to you then, to me, to you, to me, to you then...tell them Tynchy, STOP.'

The abolition of existing property relations is not at all a distinctive feature of communism
nah fam, I get it, what is yours is not mine, until you look at it Marx's way

All property relations in the past have continually been subject to historical change consequent upon the change in historical conditions
why did the anarchist drink herbal tea? because proper tea is theft (moan all you want)

The French Revolution, for example, abolished feudal property in favour of bourgeois property
the Angel of Death St Just, worked behind the scenes, sharpening his guillotine to slice off the head of King Louis the 16th

The distinguishing feature of Communism is not the abolition of property generally, but
no, no, no, we are not some kind of tabloid anarchists like Proudhon, we are for: on your Marx, get set, Gold, always disbelieve what is owned

the abolition of bourgeois property
you've not to worry about your superhero comics collection
or garden plants, it's the machines, the trains, the land, the
parliament, we want

But modern bourgeois private property is the final
the final countdown? then can I have a P please Bob? is that for
property? No, I need to go!

and most complete expression of the system of producing and
appropriating products,
'Socialism arises as a revolt against a distribution of wealth that
has lost all its moral plausibility.... The inequalities [have] become
monstrous' GBS calling for a bit of GBH I reckon!

that is based on class antagonisms, on the exploitation of the
many by the few
scum has always risen to the top, time to shake the fucking bottle,
drink up!

In this sense, the theory of the Communists may be summed up
in the single sentence
ooh, don't tell me, don't tell, let me guess...

Abolition of private property
I knew it, I knew it — tip of my tongue it was, see!

We Communists have been reproached with the desire of
abolishing the right
yes, let's abolish the Right, the right to own the spines of working
people

of personally acquiring property as the fruit of a man's own
labour
it's not so I know, because no man owns labour, just ask Corbyn,
do me a favour

[63]

which property is alleged to be the groundwork of all personal
freedom, activity and independence
a groundwork built on a swamp, time to drown them in it, innit

Hard-won, self-acquired, self-earned property!
*I think there's a no such thing coming our way, come on Karl, what
do you say?*

Do you mean the property of petty artisan and of the small
peasant, a form of property that preceded the bourgeois form?
*I never said that, but I do know all art-is-anal, when it comes from
above*

There is no need to abolish that; the development of industry
has to a great extent already destroyed it, and is still destroying it
daily.
fuck letting bygones be bygones, be gone with you

Or do you mean the modern bourgeois private property?
he has such a way with his hypophoras, do you not think?

But does wage-labour create any property for the labourer?
Err, my guess, given what has gone before, is/

Not a bit. It creates capital, i.e., that kind of property which
exploits wage-labour
*the financial bottom line has become a 24000-mile warped fan belt
wrapped around the world*

and which cannot increase except upon condition of begetting a
new supply of wage-labour for fresh exploitation.
*stem cell kidneys are coming for sale, denying the poor the ability
to sell one of theirs.*

Property, in its present form, is based on the antagonism of capital and wage labour.
look at life from both sides now, the win & lose the still somehow, life's illusions we recall, we really don't know life at all (JM remix)

Let us examine both sides of this antagonism
and we're back to the rematch of this much-anticipated bout, let's get ready to rumble!!!

To be a capitalist, is to have not only a purely personal, but a social status in production
with economic capital, comes social capital, a capital idea, what, what?

Capital is a collective product, and only by the united action of many members
just sign here, there's bingo Tuesday, Thursday, Sunday lunch, Karaoke of a Monday, & all day pass to a Saturday piss up

nay, in the last resort, only by the united action of all members of society, can it be set in motion
by the powers invested in me, I hereby declare the general public population, most honourable members of their own society

Capital is therefore not only personal; it is a social power
'I look down on him because I am upper class; I look up to him because he is upper class, but I look down on him because he is lower class; I know my place'

When, therefore, capital is converted into common property
as common as muck but as fit as fuck, so bring it

into the property of all members of society
'bagsy I get Windsor', 'fuck off twat, I'm having Sandringham then', 'ha, I think the Robert the Bruce's up there, will have a wee word or two to say about that'

[65]

Capital is therefore not only personal; it is a social power
'I look down on him because I am upper class; I look up to him because he is upper class, but I look down on him because he is lower class; I know my place'

personal property is not thereby transformed into social property
Oh, isn't it. Fair enough, didn't want a castle anyway.

It is only the social character of the property that is changed
*so fill the moat with concrete, bring down the drawbridge, no need
to rob a boat*

It loses its class character
yes, now I see — that's much better. Ooh look another money tree.

Let us now take wage-labour
*oh, go on then, if we must, but keep on like this and I'll miss my
bus*

The average price of wage-labour is the minimum wage, i.e., that
quantum of the means of subsistence
we will let the court of popular opinion determine past reparations

which is absolutely requisite to keep the labourer in bare
existence as a labourer
*but we've still got the food banks, and I'm sick of the colourless
value range*

What, therefore, the wage-labourer appropriates by means of his
labour,
*I've said it before, and I'll say it again, 'you've got to pick a pocket
or two boys', but this*

merely suffices to prolong and reproduce a bare existence
*I know, but needs must, what time's the revolution, I'm due back
at work at one*

We by no means intend to abolish this personal appropriation of
the products of labour
well thank fuck for that, I just bought these trainers, swoosh

an appropriation that is made for the maintenance and reproduction of human life
a steady state of a different kind, one that stands the test of time
and that leaves no surplus wherewith to command the labour of others
oh what a thrill when there's nothing left over for composting capital

All that we want to do away with is the miserable character of this appropriation
which finds extra hours in the day, where you go to work for no extra pay

under which the labourer lives merely to increase capital
there you go sir, do want ketchup on that fatberg?

and is allowed to live only in so far as the interest of the ruling class requires it
and they control the level of interest to suit their needs, you see

in bourgeois society, living labour is but a means to increase accumulated labour
and the way we're going they'll bring back the dead — I miss my nan

In Communist society, accumulated labour is but a means to widen
the waistbands of equality, not those of inherited banality

to enrich, to promote the existence of the labourer
who has been due more than a raise in wage, there are no echoes in an empty cage

In bourgeois society, therefore, the past dominates the present
where opportunity never knocks, no crackerjack nor good old days for this is your life

in Communist society, the present dominates the past
although we could all do with a bit more fast forward on the
remote

In bourgeois society capital is independent and has individuality
ooh, suits you sir, do you want one off the peg, or one made up,
ooh suits you sir

while the living person is dependent and has no individuality
like the interface of a ghost in its shell, organic cyber brains the
road to hell

And the abolition of this state of things is called by the
bourgeois, abolition of individuality and freedom!
the freedom to buy shares in their companies, to buy council
houses they don't own, & to keep their stupid children succeeding
without merit

And rightly so.
for there is no such thing as work sets you free

The abolition of bourgeois individuality, bourgeois
independence, and bourgeois freedom is undoubtedly aimed at
the revolution begins when individuals use bourgeois as a self-
deprecating balm across the dinner parties of London

By freedom is meant, under the present bourgeois conditions of
production, free trade, free selling and buying.
'A society can be Pareto optimal and still be perfectly disgusting.'
(AS)

But if selling and buying disappears, free selling and buying
disappears also
'Stick a pony in me pocket, I'll fetch the suitcase from the van,
cause if you want the best 'uns, and you don't ask questions, then
brother I'm your man' (JO'S)

[69]

This talk about free selling and buying, and all the other 'brave words' of our bourgeois
like the world is your jellied eel so pick yourself up, dust yourself down, your shift started five minutes ago, it's all

about freedom in general, have a meaning, if any, only in contrast with restricted selling and buying
the capitalists have put in an application to extend the day to 25 hours, they are waiting for the sun and the moon to respond

with the fettered traders of the Middle Ages,
that had local shops for local people, and sold only the 'special' stuff

but have no meaning when opposed to the Communistic abolition of buying and selling
what wasn't yours in the first place, will be everyone's in the second place

of the bourgeois conditions of production, and of the bourgeoisie itself
come and join us, come and join us, come and join us in our lair

You are horrified at our intending to do away with private property
they are absolutely horrified, just look at them: 😲

But in your existing society, private property is already done away with for nine-tenths of the population
sorry to disappoint you Karl, but it is still going some 170 years later, and it is 99% now!

its existence for the few is solely due to its non-existence in the hands of those nine-tenths
and there endeth the sequiturs (I hope)

You reproach us, therefore, with intending to do away with a
form of property
*you were lucky, in our day reproach is a social media death
sentence, visceral bots on the digital landscape*

the necessary condition for whose existence is the non-existence
of any property for the immense majority of society
there is no such thing as social mobility, just social nobility

In one word, you reproach us with intending to do away with
your property.
err, isn't that the point?

Precisely so; that is just what we intend
*I don't think our Karl would have been very good at poker, good
with a poker stick maybe*

From the moment when labour can no longer be converted into
capital, money, or rent
*we have come from cash converters to smack converters, can I see
your I.D. for your I.V.?*

into a social power capable of being monopolised
*there'll be no £200 for passing go, you're going straight to gaol,
you old knacker*

i.e., from the moment when individual property can no longer be
transformed
*come and have a look at our kitchen extension, Polish did it, lovely
chaps, slice of Royal Mazurka anyone?*

into bourgeois property, into capital, from that moment, you say,
individuality vanishes
*now you see him, now you...err, still see him – because tonight
audience, he becomes one of us!*

You must, therefore, confess that by "individual" you mean
that there's only one thing and that thing is society? Am I right?

no other person than the bourgeois, than the middle-class owner
of property
[ad break]: Marsh & Parsons have a 19th century Georgian terrace
for sale, that 'oozes' regency charm – what a facking steal!

This person must, indeed, be swept out of the way, and made
impossible
who's first then? Rees Mogg, the Johnsons, Jimmy Carr, Bear
Grylls? line them up, I've still got fairground tokens, don't be shy
you could win a coconut

Communism deprives no man of the power to appropriate the
products of society
nor women, left to translate the language of discrimination by
predators and their passives, refusing to listen

all that it does is to deprive him of the power to subjugate the
labour of others by means of such appropriations
the finders/keepers of this wealth, found it in the coffins of their
ancestors, just before the jelly set

It has been objected that upon the abolition of private property
when there is no more, 'get off my land', nor 'what time do you call
this, it's nearly dawn'

all work will cease, and universal laziness will overtake us
a bit like Newton's law of inertia? we are the force to halt
capitalism's velocity? Maybe not

According to this, bourgeois society ought long ago to have gone
to the dogs
I'll have a sky diver on trap 6 to beat 5 — I know it's a mug's game

According to this, bourgeois society ought long ago to have gone
to the dogs
I'll have a sky diver on trap 6 to beat 5 — I know it's a mug's game

through sheer idleness; for those of its members who work,
acquire nothing, and those who acquire anything do not work
a kind of arse about face way of running the economy, give what
you haven't got and we'll call it austerity

The whole of this objection is but another expression of the
tautology
pass me that do-you-think-he-saw-us, — I see, it doesn't mean the
science of teaching, nah, it's means like juggling balls one minute,
then skulls the next, it's the same innit.

that there can no longer be any wage-labour when there is no
longer any capital
I knew it was bollocks. More fake news from those who sell it,
those who fake it, those who like to own a power tower with gold
flakes on it.

All objections urged against the Communistic mode of producing
and appropriating material products
by which is meant, the chains which were ours in the first place

have, in the same way, been urged against the Communistic mode
of producing and appropriating intellectual products
the portrayals, the presses, the parliaments, the policies, the
poetry, the poetry, the poetry

Just as, to the bourgeois, the disappearance of class property is the
disappearance of production itself
don't be a mug, the guns aren't pointed at our own feet, our own
mouths, eyeballs bulging

so the disappearance of class culture is to him identical with the
disappearance of all culture
what culture? your culture! the blueprint for control, fuck your
culture (SM)

That culture, the loss of which he laments, is, for the enormous
majority, a mere training to act as a machine
Saturday night sofa bellies, pass me that line of Simon Cowell,
what time's Casualty on I could do with a good laugh

But don't wrangle with us so long as you apply, to our intended
abolition of bourgeois property, the standard of your bourgeois
notions of freedom, culture, law, &c.
your Jim Crow capitalism, colonialism, racism, sexism, ableism,
we are 'sick and tired of your ism schism & now we see the light,
we gonna stand up for our rights' (BM)

Your very ideas are but the outgrowth of the conditions of your
bourgeois production and bourgeois property
we are the knaves of the roundtable, not your panoptical subjects,
your Foucauldian power players, your tea lady waiters

just as your jurisprudence is but the will of your class made into a
law for all
the back hander, pat on the back, nod and a wink laws that lead to
SUS, stop&search, kettling, hosing, batoning, tear gas capitalism

a will whose essential character and direction are determined by
the economical conditions of existence of your class
the economy of your truth is where tongues are swabbed for
sedition, made to open wide!

The selfish misconception that induces you to transform into
eternal laws of nature and of reason
with your hands of Dogs and the wars they bring

the social forms springing from your present mode of production
and form of property
the homelessness, incurable desire for inequality, and denial of
destruction #climatechange

— historical relations that rise and disappear in the progress of production
your balls of steel clacking endlessly against each other, electric shocks zapping up against a brother

this misconception you share with every ruling class that has preceded you.
when the gloom of progress touches the end of your nose, what need of you for eyes, let us scoop them out as our prize

What you see clearly in the case of ancient property
amongst the ruins you have no care for, as heritage is not a function of war

what you admit in the case of feudal property
you refuse to believe is little worse than that which you hold dear

you are of course forbidden to admit in the case of your own bourgeois form of property
the irony that hypocrisy comes from Greek tragedy is lost on you, for you are its greatest actors, and all the world is not your stage

Abolition [Aufhebung] of the family! Even the most radical flare up at this infamous proposal of the Communists
and in such tragedies, we all know what happens to families in the end.

On what foundation is the present family, the bourgeois family, based? On capital, on private gain.
on sending your children away to be educated, you treat them like proletarians ensuring they carry on your progress

In its completely developed form, this family exists only among the bourgeoisie
but not any kind that is an example of tenderness, playfulness, guidance

But this state of things finds its complement in the practical
absence of the family among the proletarians, and in public
prostitution
for how can you call it a family when all they have in common is
work, be they adult or child

The bourgeois family will vanish as a matter of course when its
complement vanishes, and both will vanish with the vanishing of
capital
I can see clearly now the pain has gone, I can see all capitalists in
my way, gone are the long hours that had me bound, it's gonna be
a bright, bright, communist day

Do you charge us with wanting to stop the exploitation of
children by their parents?
They do, and how do you plead?

To this crime we plead guilty
order! order! the defendants have pleaded guilty to this bourgeois
accusation, I hereby sentence them to promulgate communist
values — Mr Marx, anything further you would like to say to your
bourgeois accusers? (sotto voce the Judge says: I'm sure there is
but hope there isn't)

But, you say, we destroy the most hallowed of relations, when we
replace home education by social
comparisons of destruction as a final gambit, when the enemy is
already defeated, horrifies our bourgeois judge

And your education! Is not that also social, and determined by
the social conditions under which you educate,
your playpens of the western world with their nannies and
masters, fagging hierarchy into your children at the earliest age

And your education! Is not that also social, and determined by
the social conditions under which you educate,
*your playpens of the western world with their nannies and masters,
fagging hierarchy into your children at the earliest age*

by the intervention direct or indirect, of society, by means of
schools, &c.?
*'Education in Britain is a nubile Cinderella: sparsely clad and
much interfered with' (If)*

The Communists have not invented the intervention of society in
education
*but if they did, they'd probably be the best intervenors of society in
education, PERIOD!*

they do but seek to alter the character of that intervention, and
to rescue education from the influence of the ruling class
*to stop the endless wish to test, test, test, test, who picks up a
pen after school, who sits and ticks boxes to educate themselves,
enough of your dead white males*

The bourgeois clap-trap about the family and education
*the theatrical gag, the pantomime of laughs, jaws that sag at false
applause*

about the hallowed co-relation of parents and child
one predating parental love where you send your child out to work

becomes all the more disgusting, the more, by the action of
Modern Industry
that morphs and morphs and morphs some more so that

all the family ties among the proletarians are torn asunder
keep ladling the buckets my family, else we'll go under

and their children transformed into simple articles of commerce
and instruments of labour
*if your chimney is blocked, check some child sweep isn't stuck up
there from Victorian times*

But you Communists would introduce community of women,
screams the bourgeoisie in chorus
As you will see they can introduce themselves very well thank you
not at all

The bourgeois sees his wife a mere instrument of production
what do you call bourgeois cookware that tells a wife how to cook?
Pansplaning (don't you judge me)

He hears that the instruments of production are to be exploited
in common
everyone has two ears and a mouth, so best to listen twice as much
as speaking, you hear?

and, naturally, can come to no other conclusion that the lot of
being common to all will likewise fall to the women
it seems that common sense isn't so common amongst the
bourgeoisie, you see?

He has not even a suspicion that the real point aimed at
can pierce a bourgeois brow from a distance of 12,000 words
is to do away with the status of women as mere instruments of
production

the next stop that we make will be England, tell all the folks in
Russia and China too, people all over the world, join hands, start a
love train, a love train (O'Js)

For the rest, nothing is more ridiculous than the virtuous
indignation of our bourgeois at the community of women
from death at the Epsom Derby, to Greenham Common, to #metoo

which, they pretend, is to be openly and officially established by
the Communists
I hereby declare the Prior Lives of the Rich Museum open, please
mishandle the exhibits as you wish

[80]

The Communists have no need to introduce community of
women; it has existed almost from time immemorial
hear the words of Calliope, the open scroll of Clio, beloved Erato,
the music of Euterpe, dance with Melpomene & Terpischore,
meditate with Polyhymnia, laugh with Thalia, look at the stars
with Urania, and one for luck, the poetry of Sappho

Our bourgeois, not content with having wives and daughters of
their proletarians at their disposal
Rita, with Lord Robert, and Sue too

not to speak of common prostitutes,
no, let us not speak of such capitalist enforcements, we will never
put out such endorsements

take the greatest pleasure in seducing each other's wives
Victorian key parties were all a rage, even before there were keys,
ooh look I've picked Lord Fondleme!

Bourgeois marriage is, in reality,
and your answer is [please insert]

a system of wives in common and thus
gobby wenches who will kick up a fuss?

at the most, what the Communists might possibly be reproached
with is
the mass killing of millions by dictators under its banner, or is
reproach too harsh a word? Know

that they desire to introduce, in substitution for a hypocritically
concealed, an openly legalised community of women
we see them today, in windows, street corners, once on cards in
phone boxes, all over that internet

For the rest, it is self-evident that the abolition of the present system of production
where people get high on their own supply, puts out their brain's fire

must bring with it the abolition of the community of women springing from that system, i.e., of prostitution both public and private
whether one or the other, victims both of gender based violence, daughter, sister, aunt or mother

The Communists are further reproached with desiring to abolish countries and nationality
In God we Trust, God bless, God Save, from sea to sea, Vive la, Unity-Discipline-labour, by giving mercy and by choosing, Wales forever!

The working men have no country. We cannot take from them what they have not got
dum spiro spero — while I breathe I hope, unity in diversity, out of many, one people (irie)

Since the proletariat must first of all acquire political supremacy, must rise
like lions after slumber, in unvanquishable number (PBS)

to be the leading class of the nation, must constitute itself the nation
one nation under a groove, getting down just for the funk of it, nothing can stop us now

it is so far, itself national, though not in the bourgeois sense of the word
that sense that everyone's a stranger, everyone's a danger, guns at the ready to kill your neighbour

National differences and antagonism between peoples are daily
more and more vanishing
as gluttony trumps envy, as greed trumps need, as pride takes you
for a ride

owing to the development of the bourgeoisie, to freedom of
commerce, to the world market
of container ships and drones, we've got a delivery package for
you, think you want it, you've got it!

to uniformity in the mode of production and in the conditions of
life corresponding thereto
in other words, hydra-headed, toilet papering, data diddling,
cyber-secure evidencing

The supremacy of the proletariat will cause them to vanish still
faster
the top hats and tails, the royal parades, we'll dig out our spades,
super highways

United action,
United or any one, they shan't defeat us, we'll fight till the game is
won! (#pusb)

of the leading civilised countries at least
best to start at the top with a bottom up approach, here watch my
PowerPoint legislation

is one of the first conditions for the emancipation of the
proletariat
if we wanna be the best, then we gotta beat the rest, emancipation
is what we need

In proportion, as the exploitation of one individual by another
will also be put an end to
The last trumpet ever to be sounded shall blow even algebra to
wreck (CD)

the exploitation of one nation by another will also be put an end
to
smell will be given back its sense so it can taste the delights of
others, shared platters

In proportion, as the antagonism between classes within the
nation vanishes
use of the word antagonism rose exponentially from the 1850s,
sad to say it remains at high levels today #justsaying

the hostility of one nation to another will come to an end.
the horizons of hostility still burn with the nuclear ghost, a cancer
cell of opportunity

The charges against Communism made from a religious
Holy Mary, Mother of God, pray for us sinners, now and at the
hour of our death

a philosophical and, generally, from an ideological standpoint
you may accuse Marx of calling the kettle black here, but his
ideological pot is Grade A

are not deserving of serious examination
shall we test them anyway, let's start with their children like they
do ours, what's the meaning of life, I'll give you a clue, what's 6x7?

Does it require deep intuition to comprehend that
try tripping your feet down a poor person's street, and you will see
a woman's and

a man's ideas, views, and conception, in one word, man's
consciousness
whether that be from above or below, it is not what you believe, it
is all that you know

All resistance is a rupture with what is. And every rupture begins, for those engaged in it, through a rupture with oneself."
(Alain Badiou).

changes with every change in the conditions of his material existence,
to stand out as a crowd, not to stand out in it, as you well know —
you have to be in it to win it

in his social relations and in his social life?
between mother and son, father and daughter, women and men,
men and men, women and women, them and they

What else does the history of ideas prove,
how can we know anything from catechisms and rote, made to
learn life through other peoples' quotes

than that intellectual production changes its character in proportion as material production is changed?
by doing away with out of tune algorithms, we can hear ourselves
think in time of our measure

The ruling ideas of each age have ever been the ideas of its ruling class
at the start were the Iroquois and primitive communism, then
came the ages of the slave, feudal, capitalist, who layered people
like paupers' graves

When people speak of the ideas that revolutionise society,
listen, are you breathing just a little, calling it a life? (MO)

they do but express that fact that within the old society the elements of a new one have been created
progress is a restive mind, mining dust motes for humankind

and that the dissolution of the old ideas keeps even pace with the dissolution of the old conditions of existence
how can we save our girls and boys from Oppenheimer's deadly
toys (GS)

[86]

When the ancient world was in its last throes, the ancient
religions were overcome by Christianity.
*the progeny of stale bread binds the ingredients for Christmas
pudding*

When Christian ideas succumbed in the 18th century to
rationalist ideas
*give us this day, our daily bread, but forgive us our debts is not
what we said*

feudal society fought its death battle with the then revolutionary
bourgeoisie
everyone's a revolutionary until they grow out of their T-shirt

The ideas of religious liberty and freedom of conscience
ones that remain to this day, and cannot be told to go away

merely gave expression to the sway of free competition within the
domain of knowledge
pouring oil on troubled waters only adds heat to rising tensions

"Undoubtedly," it will be said
*the sixth amendment of the US constitution states: 'the accused
shall enjoy the right...to be confronted with the witnesses against
him' — so Carry on Karl*

religious, moral, philosophical, and juridical ideas have been
modified in the course of historical development.
and so they have, so what of it?

But religion, morality, philosophy, political science, and law,
constantly survived this change
*Yes, but aren't you forgetting something, no? give him a sec,
nearly there*

The delights of western democracy are there for all to consume

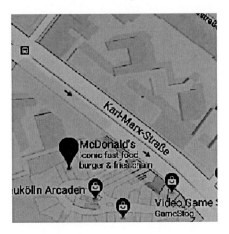

At the fall of the Berlin Wall, a reporter asked a young man who had crossed from the East for the first time: "What are you most looking forward to with your new-found freedom?" To which the man replied, "Buying a pair of Levi jeans and a pack of Marlboro cigarettes."

There are, besides, eternal truths, such as Freedom, Justice, etc.,
that are common to all states of society
we can agree that all states of society have in common inequality

But Communism abolishes eternal truths, it abolishes all
religion, and all morality
j'accuse 'the aim is to enlighten those who have been kept in the
dark, in the name of humanity' (EZ)

instead of constituting them on a new basis; it therefore acts in
contradiction to all past historical experience
non, non, non, the ruling class is a man with a thousand faces,
everyone the same (allo, allo, allo)

What does this accusation reduce itself to?
a front page splash by tabloid trash, flash the cash but don't be
rash

The history of all past society has consisted in the development
of class antagonisms
the will to power is Nietzsche's ruse, to find meaning in suffering
is no excuse

antagonisms that assumed different forms at different epochs
Thessalonica, the French September, Auschwitz, Nanking, Mai
Lai, Rwanda, Halabja, Srebrenica, museums of ad nauseum

But whatever form they may have taken, one fact is common to
all past ages, viz.
which wasn't a bad comic, although the Fat Slags got a bad press

the exploitation of one part of society by the other.
'this earth is a trophy cup for the industrious man...He who does
not possess the force to secure his Lebensraum in this world...does
not deserve to possess the necessities of life' (AH) Fuck off!

No wonder, then, that the social consciousness of past ages,
despite all the multiplicity and variety it displays,
in the uncertain time of white dogs, cynics offered freedom and
happiness to stop us all from going, well, to the dogs

moves within certain common forms, or general ideas
a 24 hour watershed of soft power headlines, prime times, clothes
lines, don't you dare step out of line

which cannot completely vanish except with the total
disappearance of class antagonisms
when the balance between normal microbiota and pathogenic
microbes is antagonised, we have a problem

The Communist revolution is the most radical rupture with
traditional property relations
Kuhn showed that progress is not 'steady as you go', it is a process
of disruption/ turmoil/ overthrow

no wonder that its development involved the most radical rupture
with traditional ideas
I know, but after all we've been through, what have we to show?

But let us have done with the bourgeois objections to
Communism
never to forgive them for they know exactly what they do

We have seen above, that the first step in the revolution by the
working class
once they've put their bet on and won a line of bingo

is to raise the proletariat to the position of ruling class to win the
battle of democracy
that bluntest of rules, that keeper of the Faith, that steady as you
go, that resultant of death

The proletariat will use its political supremacy to wrest, by
degree, all capital from the bourgeoisie
we are more than hard work can't you see, we are more than
surviving worker bees

to centralise all instruments of production in the hands of the
State,
we are more than dire poverty, so we've come to smash the dying
bourgeoisie

i.e., of the proletariat organised as the ruling class; and to
increase the total productive forces as rapidly as possible
only those who have limited means, truly know how to organise
themselves

Of course, in the beginning, this cannot be effected except by
means of despotic inroads
history has shown the folly of this, the too quick, too strict, the
don't worry 'I've got this'

on the rights of property, and on the conditions of bourgeois
production
so 'stand by your beds', 'empty your pockets', 'did you pack this
bag yourself, enjoy your flight'

by means of measures, therefore, which appear economically
insufficient and untenable, but which,
GDP was a false measure, the Japanese will tell you, when the
Kobe earthquake struck, the cost of reconstruction saw GDP go
up

in the course of the movement, outstrip themselves, necessitate
further inroads upon the old social order
the bourgeoisie will melt into the foreground, for there will be no
background anymore

and are unavoidable as a means of entirely revolutionising the mode of production
take it away Ken (don't sing this in a French accent), 'Happiness, Happiness, the greatest gift that I possess, I've got no silver and I've got no gold, just a whole lot of happiness in my soul (KD)

These measures will, of course, be different in different countries
the US to Canada, UK to EU, South Africa to Mozambique, the Philippines to Japan, Saudi Arabia to Iran, to the weight of all things

Nevertheless, in most advanced countries, the following will be
pretty generally applicable
*so behold, the secular ten commandments, scribed in the original
Manifest der kommunistischen Partei*

Communism's Ten Commandments

1. Abolition of property in land and application of all rents of land to public purpose
I suggest we begin with cutting the hedge funds, the casino capitalism, the prospecting close your eyes and pick a card path to prosperity

2. A heavy progressive or graduated income tax
in the heated climate of today's reprobates, they'll not be much need for public debate

3. Abolition of all rights of inheritance
Can I keep my granddad's watch, it's broken, it's worthless, it means a lot?

4. Confiscation of the property of all emigrants and rebels
there'll be no more capital flight, those runways closed at midnight

5. Centralisation of credit in the hands of the state, by means of a national bank with State capital and an exclusive monopoly
credit where credit is due, an economy not founded on a global debt of $233 trillion, phew!

6. Centralisation of the means of communication and transport in the hands of the State
yes traveller I'm just putting you through, can you believe it no trains overdue

7. Extension of factories and instruments of production owned by the State
of factories, mere metal filings remain, big data now is the name of the game

the bringing into cultivation of waste-lands, and the
improvement of the soil generally in accordance with a common
plan
*I sat upon the shore/ Fishing, with the arid plain behind me/ Shall
I at least set my lands in order (TSE)*

8. Equal liability of all to work. Establishment of industrial
armies, especially for agriculture
*you might need a little marketing advice, industrial armies doesn't
sound nice*

9. Combination of agriculture with manufacturing industries;
gradual abolition of all the distinction between town and country
by a more equable distribution of the populace over the country
*the green with the grey, cosmopolitan hue, no borders, no
hoarders, no get in the queue*

10. Free education for all children in public schools. Abolition
of children's factory labour in its present form. Combination of
education with industrial production, &c, &c.
*with child labour, girls denied education, we mustn't forget this is
not done and dusted, those wheels have not come off yet, though
they may be a little rusted*

****

When, in the course of development, class distinctions have
disappeared
*no more rabbit in the hat, hamster on a wheel, no beggar thy
neighbour, from which we did steal*

and all production has been concentrated in the hands of a vast
association of the whole nation
*One thing I can tell you is you got to be free, Come together right
now over me (L&Mc)*

the public power will lose its political character. Political power, properly so called
hard boiled sweet, soft in the middle, bite too soon, swallow the glass and glitter

is merely the organised power of one class for oppressing another
#FunMythAsPolemic: birds without wings are twice as likely to peck your greedy eyes out, feast on the bleed

If the proletariat during its contest with the bourgeoisie is compelled, by the force of circumstances
a contest is it? no looking at your phones to find the answers then, this is not a pub quiz

to organise itself as a class, if, by means of a revolution, it makes itself the ruling class
Emancipate yourselves from mental slavery, None but ourselves can free our minds, Have no fear for atomic energy, 'Cause none of them can stop the time (BM)

and, as such, sweeps away by force the old conditions of production
Trigger's broom will do it, once you ask yourself the philosophical question, is anything original?

then it will, along with these conditions, have swept away the conditions for the existence of class antagonisms and of classes generally
(we are getting to the point where a cost/benefit analysis of 'hammering the point home' would come in handy)

and will thereby have abolished its own supremacy as a class
witness the fitness as we abolish the polish, say class not clarse (unless east end), hold the chain whilst we swamp the drain

In place of the old bourgeois society, with its classes and class antagonisms, we shall have an association
I hereby call this revolution to order, I guess there's a Slim Shady in all of us, Fuck it, Let's all stand up

in which the free development of each is the condition for the free development of all.
We'll do the twist, the stomp, the mashed potato too, Any old dance that you wanna do, But let's dance, well let's dance (CC)

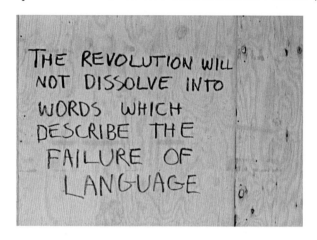

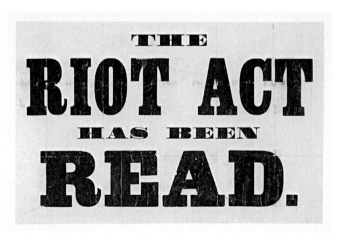

Part Three

Socialist and Communist Literature

Part Three. Socialist and Communist Literature

1. Reactionary Socialism

A. Feudal Socialism
Owing to their historical position, it became the vocation of the
aristocracies of France and England
those Macaroni fops with their tubular wigs, white frilly chests,
one two buckle my shoe you knave, began

to write pamphlets against modern bourgeois society
pamphlet wars influenced the populace for decades, as today's
vox poppets try to do in spades

In the French Revolution of July 1830, and in the English reform
agitation, these aristocracies again succumbed to the hateful
upstart
funny to think of capitalists as upstarts, now their teeth frenzy
on a meat free bone

Thenceforth, a serious political struggle was altogether out of the
question
the scene is set, aristocrats bow to political change, what next,
armed resistance? we're ready Karl

A literary battle alone remained possible.
what? So we sharpen our pencils and poke the eye with the page,
is that it?

But even in the domain of literature the old cries of the
restoration period had become impossible
placards and songs from the unwashed throngs, 'the Republic
calls us/...a Frenchman must live for her/ for her a Frenchman
must die'

In order to arouse sympathy, the aristocracy was obliged to lose sight, apparently, of its own interests
but only apparently, for their sight, although a long one, was kept alive looking toward a short-term strategy

and to formulate their indictment against the bourgeoisie in the interest of the exploited working class alone.
the top with the bottom, united to force the 'squeezed middle' to burst the countries' boil

Thus, the aristocracy took their revenge by singing lampoons
'everybody wants to be a cat, because a cat's the only cat, who knows where it's at, everybody's picking up on that feline beat, cause everything else is obsolete'

on their new masters and whispering in his ears sinister prophesies of coming catastrophe.
"From the enslaved populace,/ songs, Chants and demands/ While princes and lords are held captive in prisons./ These will in the future by headless idiots/ Be received as divine prayers." (N)

In this way arose feudal Socialism: half lamentation, half lampoon; half an echo of the past, half menace of the future;
four halves, makes two wholes, past & present, Carlyle & Disraeli, a double act of reactionary backs bent double against change

at times, by its bitter, witty and incisive criticism, striking the bourgeoisie to the very heart's core
In Coningsby Disraeli did summon up such stasis, 'A government of statesmen or of clerks? Of Humbug or Humdrum?'

but always ludicrous in its effect, through total incapacity to comprehend the march of modern history.
'you can never hold back Spring, I will never stop believing... winter dreams the same dream every time, the world is dreaming, dreaming of Spring' (TW)

The aristocracy, in order to rally the people to them, waved the proletarian alms-bag in front for a banner.
got any pennies mate? Yes young trog, but you must keep to your hovel, agreed? Now go on, grovel!

But the people, so often as it joined them, saw on their hindquarters the old feudal coats of arms, and deserted with loud and irreverent laughter.
ha, ha, ha, it's the three lions on your shirt, all over again, but no-one can hold their breath for that long

One section of the French Legitimists and "Young England" exhibited this spectacle
looking back at Salic Law they thought they were winning, heads at 180, inheritance was a dirty nappy left to the women

In pointing out that their mode of exploitation was different to that of the bourgeoisie
what type of exploitation can we help you with today serf? we've still got the stocks, and the tomatoes are extra ripe this time of year

the feudalists forget that they exploited under circumstances and conditions that were quite different and that are now antiquated
excuse me for a minute pleb, I have a bit of competition I have to deal with, unhand my ermine sir!

In showing that, under their rule, the modern proletariat never existed, they forget that the modern bourgeoisie is the necessary offspring of their own form of society
we feudals will have sex with anything we see, Serf or TERF but never the bourgeoisie.

For the rest, so little do they conceal the reactionary character of their criticism
they'll be no peek a boo, nor other such games, but look very closely & you'll see what we've made

that their chief accusation against the bourgeois amounts to this,
a hill of beans, a shilling in a shoe, the thrill of a bill, they'll be no tips for you

that under the bourgeois régime a class is being developed
a class of people who on the surface look as dirty and apathetic as the dogs that they keep

which is destined to cut up root and branch the old order of society
but the bourgeois chamois shows that their sheen is virile

What they upbraid the bourgeoisie with is not so much that it creates a proletariat as that it creates a revolutionary proletariat
for the love of god, can that really be true, close the gates call your mates, WTF should we do

In political practice, therefore, they join in all coercive measures against the working class
with the blunt tools of the Peelers, the Bobbies, the Beasts, from Peterloo to Orgreave people keep bleeding

and in ordinary life, despite their high-falutin phrases
those goddam rooting tooting high-falutin, I can't understand any of that shinnery diggery

they stoop to pick up the golden apples dropped from the tree of industry
the raven watches as they take a bite, with no first love kiss to help in sight

and to barter truth, love, and honour, for traffic in wool,
beetroot-sugar, and potato spirits
oh blood hearted beetroot, shall I compare thee to a summer's
day, thou art more finite than abstract nouns, I must have thee in
whatever way

As the parson has ever gone hand in hand with the landlord
skipping through the fields, killing all the weeds

so has Clerical Socialism with Feudal Socialism
against poverty, idolatry, a life based on a lottery, is where the
difference is riven

Nothing is easier than to give Christian asceticism a Socialist
tinge.
'The Labour party has never been a socialist party, although
there have always been socialists in it - a bit like Christians in the
Church of England.' (TB)

Has not Christianity declaimed against private property, against
marriage, against the State?
though they make such a lot of money from all three, pennies
from the penniless

Has it not preached in the place of these, charity and poverty,
celibacy and mortification of the flesh, monastic life and Mother
Church?
such asceticism is a battle for last place, and celibacy has
consequence for the human race

Christian Socialism is but the holy water with which the priest
consecrates the heart-burnings of the aristocrat.
the twin tracks of moral dualism can carry the same train, with
first class at the front and rear

B. Petty-Bourgeois Socialism

The feudal aristocracy was not the only class that was ruined by
the bourgeoisie
what's left of their leaky estates is propped up by English Heritage,
the National Trust

not the only class whose conditions of existence pined and
perished in the atmosphere of modern bourgeois society
places can be quietly crowded without the diverse being heard

The medieval burgesses and the small peasant proprietors were
the precursors of the modern bourgeoisie.
late night corner shop, that light to the sale of skins, cheap cider, a
chat behind the counter

In those countries which are but little developed
yes, developed has become such a contested term, its domestic
product must always be gross

industrially and commercially, these two classes still vegetate side
by side with the rising bourgeoisie
so they cogitate each end of the scales, searching their cupboards
for reason

In countries where modern civilisation has become fully
developed
in my office Karl! We need to talk about the term civilisation, I'll
bring you up to date

a new class of petty bourgeois has been formed, fluctuating
between proletariat and bourgeoisie
these P-Bs really are a mixed bunch, from the multi-coloured fruit
& veg shops of Asia and Africa

A new class of petty bourgeoisie has formed....ever renewing itself
to hipster cereal and coffee bars where you can hang your bike on the end of the owner's moustache

and ever renewing itself as a supplementary part of bourgeois society.
to hipster cereal and coffee bars where you can hang your bike on the end of the owner's moustache

The individual members of this class, however, are being constantly hurled down
war in a Babylon, tribal war in a Babylon, let me tell, it sipple out deh

into the proletariat by the action of competition, and, as modern industry develops
& bwoy has it developed, with the showers in their towers, and the secret password shibboleth

they even see the moment approaching when they will completely disappear as an independent section of modern society,
they ain't gone yet bruv, but they're breathing air from an upturned boat.

to be replaced in manufactures, agriculture and commerce, by overlookers, bailiffs and shopmen
can't pay, we'll take it away, nightmare tenants, scum landlords, food bank parties, tax invaders

In countries like France, where the peasants constitute far more than half of the population
now French dudes know how to protest, how to look after their dwindling rights in crowded airspace

it was natural that writers
there's nothing natural about writers, nor should there be

who sided with the proletariat against the bourgeoisie should use, in their criticism of the bourgeois régime
swear words are good, they make their point succinctly, piercingly,

acutely, without such abstraction, e.g. jog on you [insert swear word]

the standard of the peasant and petty bourgeois
in a swear fair I know who would win the coconut, the sickly gold fish, the fuck-off cuddly toy

and from the standpoint of these intermediate classes, should take up the cudgels for the working class.
a question to ask ourselves today, what are we to think of the middle; there is speaking for & there is speaking with

Thus arose petty-bourgeois Socialism.
the monk Dom Perignon could not rid the Abbey's wine of its bubbles, 'I am drinking the stars' he exclaimed, thus the champagne of socialists was born.

Sismondi was the head of this school, not only in France but also in England
he told that an economy has perpetual hills, between which we must cycle, clip clip

This school of Socialism dissected with great acuteness the contradictions in the conditions of modern production.
an agreement of diagnosis does not translate into remedy; herbal root or operation, palliative or cure

It laid bare the hypocritical apologies of economists
those who wept like crocodiles over the bloody meat of progress

It proved, incontrovertibly, the disastrous effects of machinery and division of labour
Smith had said, the worker naturally loses, 'the habit of such exertion, and generally becomes as stupid and ignorant as it is possible for a human creature to become (AS).

the concentration of capital and land in a few hands;
overproduction and crises;
they lay their tied moneybags across the table, like wontons
stuffed with truffles

it pointed out the inevitable ruin of the petty bourgeois and
peasant
at the bust of a cycle, a patch on a puncture will not do when there
is no bike to fix

the misery of the proletariat, the anarchy in production
as if they weren't miserable enough, some turn to a more
productive kind of anarchy

the crying inequalities in the distribution of wealth
we don't want to share our tears, they are lines of memories that
fight the fears

the industrial war of extermination between nations
Tommy gun, You'll be dead when your war is won, Tommy gun,
But did you have to gun down everyone? (TC)

the dissolution of old moral bonds, of the old family relations,
of the old nationalities.
we've sold the old, the bold, the cold, if truth be told, all we hold,
are brittle flakes of fools' gold

In its positive aims, however,
these clever Trevors have come with their white-flecked overalls to
paint and paper the rotting walls

this form of Socialism aspires either to restoring the old means
of production and of exchange
as seen in last week's episode of the Antiques Roadshow, where
Fiona Bruce was for once dumbfounded

and with them the old property relations, and the old society
a country pile going cheap, entitlements not included

or to cramping the modern means of production and of exchange
The Wicked Witch may not have said, 'fly my pretties, fly' — but
the mass memory discrepancy effect still has all the wings

within the framework of the old property relations that have
been, and were bound to be, exploded by those means
you don't remember remember the 5th of November? That's
because there's much more money in Halloween, coming from the
United States of Mean

In either case, it is both reactionary and Utopian
the future's bright, the future's orange, because nothing Trumps
the rhymes of orange

Its last words are: corporate guilds for manufacture; patriarchal
relations in agriculture
that divide has long since gone, just another thing they got wrong

Ultimately, when stubborn historical facts had dispersed all
intoxicating effects of self-deception
When will that be? Say the bells of Stepney. I do not know, Says
the bell-end of Bow. Here comes a candle to light you to bed, And
here comes a chopper to chop off your head!

his form of Socialism ended in a miserable fit of the blues
in Germany, where we go to now, to have the blues is to be drunk,
I'll drink to that, Zum Wohl!

C. German or "True" Socialism

The Socialist and Communist literature of France
*dans L'Industrie of Saint-Simon, l'Utopian Fourier, et le mutual
anarchist, Proudhon*

a literature that originated under the pressure of a bourgeoisie in
power
*of Napolean's First French Empire, the conservative Bourbons, and
the long July of Louis Philippe*

and that was the expressions of the struggle against this power,
was introduced into Germany at a time when
*they were then a weak set of states in 1815, soft around the edges,
eager to congeal in parity*

the bourgeoisie, in that country, had just begun its contest with
feudal absolutism
French power and annexation helped spur this nascent sparring

German philosophers, would-be philosophers, and beaux esprits
(men of letters), eagerly seized on this literature
French theory to German practice, span around a different axis

only forgetting, that when these writings immigrated from France
into Germany
*a blood-stained westerly wind, helped stick the pages to
intellectual faces*

French social conditions had not immigrated along with them
*for there was little you could call German, as Austria and Prussia
called all the shots*

In contact with German social conditions
inalienable, fractured, frozen, melting

this French literature lost all its immediate practical significance
and assumed a purely literary aspect
that most romantic of reactions, where a fireside revolution is a
perfect night cap

Thus, to the German philosophers of the Eighteenth Century
Goethe had it right: 'knowing is not enough; we must apply.
Willing is not enough, we must do'

the demands of the first French Revolution were nothing more
than the demands of "Practical Reason" in general
an enlightened response, which in the eyes of Pinker is seen as
non-negotiable, so take that you ancient regimes!

and the utterance of the will of the revolutionary French
bourgeoisie signified
that the bourgeois sense of enlightenment comes an overblown
sense of entitlement, 'err I think you'll find that's my parking
space'

in their eyes, the laws of pure Will, of Will as it was bound to be,
of true human Will generally
they were antonyms of the akrastic, for to go against reason and
will, was to go against oneself

The work of the German literati consisted solely in bringing the
new French ideas into harmony with their ancient philosophical
conscience
thus they were forever ibid, op cit., that's what mes amis said, to
which they agreed mit Ja

or rather, in annexing the French ideas without deserting their
own philosophic point of view
they became an appendix to the annex, and theirs grumbled along
in their mother tongue

[113]

As an artist I come to sing, but as a citizen, I will always speak for peace, and no one can silence me in this.
(Paul Robeson)

This annexation took place in the same way in which a foreign language is appropriated, namely, by translation
"Freiheit, Gleichheit, Brüderlichkeit oder Tod; — die letzte, am einfachsten zu geben, O Guillotine! " (CD)

It is well known how the monks wrote silly lives of Catholic Saints
well they have a lot of time on their hands when they are not clasped in prayer

over the manuscripts on which the classical works of ancient heathendom had been written
we heathens without such classical education, wrote life in the darkness of our caves

The German literati reversed this process with the profane French literature
back to life, back to surreality, back to the here and then, yeah (S2S)

They wrote their philosophical nonsense beneath the French original
peel back the wallpaper of history, and it is not only badly drawn cocks that will give you a shock

For instance, beneath the French criticism of the economic functions of money, they wrote "Alienation of Humanity"
in your own word Karl Gattungswesen, the nature of us as a species is moulded

and beneath the French criticism of the bourgeois state they wrote "Dethronement of the Category of the General", and so forth.
smooth-talking philosophers of Germany unite, you have nothing to lose but the heavy weight of your vocabulary

The introduction of these philosophical phrases at the back of the
French historical criticisms
you could say were not going to be for ad agencies, adbusters?
maybe

they dubbed "Philosophy of Action", "True Socialism", "German
Science of Socialism", "Philosophical Foundation of Socialism",
and so on
a comparative analysis of national turbulence and its influence on
intellectual language is worth a commission here

The French Socialist and Communist literature was thus
completely emasculated
though I'm not sure they cared so much, as they had a full plate of
shit to disgust

And, since it ceased in the hands of the German to express the
struggle of one class with the other
only one type of bias can there be, and it cannot come from one
country

he felt conscious of having overcome "French one-sidedness"
the union of any Europe has more than twenty seven sides, but
some are longer than others

and of representing, not true requirements, but the requirements
of Truth
it was once said there are no facts, only interpretations (N), today
there are no fictions, just distortions

not the interests of the proletariat, but the interests of Human
Nature
sometimes people do the strangest things, so let the carnival begin,
every pleasure every sin (GC)

of Man in general, who belongs to no class, has no reality, who
exists only in the misty realm of philosophical fantasy
*pick a card any card, now put it back in the pack, go on! It doesn't
fit, does it? Well how about that?*

This German socialism, which took its schoolboy task so
seriously and solemnly
*ouch, Karl does not hold back, when it comes to fellow country
folk*

and extolled its poor stock-in-trade in such a mountebank
fashion, meanwhile gradually lost its pedantic innocence
*say what you see: app + rent + ice, equals the square route of a
group who are viewed as not so bright*

The fight of the Germans, and especially of the Prussian
bourgeoisie
*the Germans were not always united, many were caught stealing
a slice of their own kuchen*

against feudal aristocracy and absolute monarchy, in other
words, the liberal movement, became more earnest
*the business case for socialism was starting to take hold, the 1815
Vienna Congress was said to be to blame for this, but the German
move into the socialist fold, was a case of hit and miss*

By this, the long-wished for opportunity was offered to "True"
Socialism
*I wonder if Karl ever did the "air quote" thing, it would have made
a dream of a meme*

of confronting the political movement with the Socialist
demands
*insiders outsiders upside downsiders, where they will end, nobody
knows (or cares?)*

of hurling the traditional anathemas against liberalism
the sewage dredgers of profit

against representative government
the keepers of a safe distance

against bourgeois competition
the oligops & monopolots

bourgeois freedom of the press
the say it don't spray it type of news

bourgeois legislation, bourgeois liberty and equality
the do as I naysay, sprinkled with hope dust along the way

and of preaching to the masses that they had nothing to gain,
and everything to lose, by this bourgeois movement
*which school bully do you prefer? The one who steals your lunch
money, or the one who steals your mind*

German Socialism forgot, in the nick of time
*ooh, I just remembered, I mustn't forget something I mustn't
forget*

that the French criticism, whose silly echo it was
*encased in a chamber so reverberative it can still be heard in the
19th Convocation of the National Congress of China*

presupposed the existence of modern bourgeois society
*who goes there? Bourgeois, you say? Then show us your
credentials — Anti-bourgeois Express? ooh, that'll do nicely sir*

with its corresponding economic conditions of existence and the
political constitution adapted thereto
*the square mile never really wanted to fit into the round hole, but
analogies are analogies that sometimes become realities*

the very things whose attainment was the object of the pending struggle in Germany
we have a match ladies and gentlemen, so let the battle commence ad finitum

To the absolute governments, with their following of parsons, professors, country squires, and officials,
those conduits of collusion, whose nests were a feathered duck down or we'll blow your bloody wings off

it served as a welcome scarecrow against the threatening bourgeoisie
so they'd while away the hours, conferin' with the flowers, consultin' with the rain, their heads would be scratchin' while their thoughts were busy hatchin', if they only had a brain (WofO)

It was a sweet finish, after the bitter pills of flogging and bullets
I may be beaten, I may be browed, but that christmas pudding, makes me want to sing out loud

with which these same governments, just at that time, dosed the German working-class risings
whether Lord or Magnate, the powerful hand out beatings like they hand out gruel

While this "True" Socialism thus served the government as a weapon for fighting the German bourgeoisie
when you are at the top, it is a puzzle to be stuck in the middle, between two arse cheeks from below

it, at the same time, directly represented a reactionary interest, the interest of German Philistines.
these Spiessbürgers were seen as wee timorous beasties, with the panic of change burning their breastie (RB)

[119]

In Germany, the petty-bourgeois class, a relic of the sixteenth century
who occasionally dusted themselves off, when the chance of advancement took them out of their trough

and since then constantly cropping up again under the various forms is the real social basis of the existing state of things.
who amidst the turbulence of the country's disfigurement kept their place with the soothing balm of local reform

To preserve this class is to preserve the existing state of things in Germany
a ghost's rasp hawks the phlegm of change, a spew of the old mixed with chunks from the new

The industrial and political supremacy of the bourgeoisie threatens it with certain destruction
The King is in the altogether, but altogether, the altogether, He's altogether as naked as the day that he was born (FL)

— on the one hand, from the concentration of capital
that monkey wrench to the skull

on the other, from the rise of a revolutionary proletariat.
that straight down the middle, kick in the balls

"True" Socialism appeared to kill these two birds with one stone
no-one knows who threw it first, but now they're all at it with a wretched thirst

It spread like an epidemic
we must remember that an epidemic was not enough, but a pandemic across borders was going to be tough

[120]

The robe of speculative cobwebs, embroidered with flowers of rhetoric, steeped in the dew of sickly sentiment
wreaths of change gave a light hue to Germany's winter, with shoots of yellow and red, but also black

this transcendental robe in which the German Socialists wrapped their sorry "eternal truths"
this Kantian cape, covered with the stains of God's activity still guiding human morality

all skin and bone, served to wonderfully increase the sale of their goods amongst such a public.
but a heart that pumps the blood, is nothing without a spleen from which to vent

And on its part German Socialism recognised, more and more, its own calling as the bombastic representative of the petty-bourgeois Philistine
they may look like idiots, talk like idiots, but don't let that fool you. They really are idiots (GM)

It proclaimed the German nation to be the model nation, and the German petty Philistine to be the typical man.
proclaim away, but we won't walk five hundred miles, no we won't walk five hundred more, to be the proles that fall down at your door

To every villainous meanness of this model man, it gave a hidden, higher, Socialistic interpretation, the exact contrary of its real character.
cloak and dagger, swish and swagger, big & bold, forever the bragger

It went to the extreme length of directly opposing the "brutally destructive" tendency of Communism and of proclaiming its supreme and impartial contempt of all class struggles.
the extremities of such lengths, mixed with cold tendencies, saw the limbs of their arguments drop off into the hot vat of verbiage

With very few exceptions, all the so-called Socialist and Communist publications that now (1847) circulate in Germany belong to the domain of this foul and enervating literature
But one year on, revolutions brought to an end such sick-lit solutions

2. Conservative or Bourgeois Socialism

A part of the bourgeoisie is desirous of redressing social grievances
it is the ankles, where the sewage of poverty swells at their swill

in order to secure the continued existence of bourgeois society
but instead of lowering the waters, they pull on their boots

To this section belong economists
macro, micro, meso, econometrists, game theorists, gamblers, tramps & thieves

philanthropists
from Thomas Coram & Octavia Hill, to George Soros & Bill Gates

humanitarians
the blankets, tents, camps, stomach fillers, pain killers

improvers of the condition of the working class
who gave a person a fish, but never the rod

The bourgeoisie naturally conceives the world in which it is
supreme to be the best
*'democracy is the worst form of Government except for all those
other forms that have been tried from time to time' (WC) – still
shit tho', innit*

organisers of charity
complicit palliatives of a corrupt system, never the challengers,
always the laggers

members of societies for the prevention of cruelty to animals
hence the predominance of cats on social media

temperance fanatics
Let's raise a glass to them, slainte

hole-and-corner reformers of every imaginable kind
bless them all, fuck them all, the long, the short and the tall, you'll
get no promotion this side of the ocean, so let's keep singing fuck
them all

This form of socialism has, moreover, been worked out into
complete systems.
testing, testing, 3-2-1, we have lift off, all systems go, as in go away

We may cite Proudhon's Philosophie de la Misère as an example
of this form
liberty comes 'from the bowels of the people, from the depths of
labour, a greater authority, a more potent fact, which shall envelop
capital and the state and subjugate them'

The Socialistic bourgeois want all the advantages of modern
social conditions without the struggles and dangers necessarily
resulting therefrom
even with boots and gloves to protect the skin, but the mud and the
scum are not for him

They desire the existing state of society, minus its revolutionary
and disintegrating elements.
they think we can rise together with their tax credits in a free
market, but it is merely the botox in a wrinkled economy.

They wish for a bourgeoisie without a proletariat
but who will clean their houses, who will clean their kids, who will
salve their conscience, for all the good they did

The bourgeoisie naturally conceives the world in which it is
supreme to be the best
'democracy is the worst form of Government except for all those
other forms that have been tried from time to time' (WC) – still
shit tho', innit

and bourgeois Socialism develops this comfortable conception
into various more or less complete systems
a watch, whether analogue or digital, still has its working parts
hidden out back

In requiring the proletariat to carry out such a system, and
thereby to march straightway into the social New Jerusalem
across the green and pleasant lands of a plenty for few, and a few
for plenty

it but requires in reality, that the proletariat should remain
within the bounds of existing society
stand by your beds you 'orrible little lot, today is your lucky day,
a small ration of luxury is on its way

but should cast away all its hateful ideas concerning the
bourgeoisie
so if you have anything to say, say it now or forever hold your
piece of shit life you hold in your hands right now

A second, and more practical, but less systematic, form of this
Socialism
like rifles, this is but one kind of socialism, there are many like it,
but this one is mine

sought to depreciate every revolutionary movement in the eyes of
the working class
*My socialism and I know that what counts in war is not the rounds
we fire, the noise of our burst, nor the smoke we make. We know
that it is the hits that count.*

by showing that no mere political reform
*widening the franchise, strengthening the unions, minimizing the
misery,*

but only a change in the material conditions of existence
with bigger ties, higher heels, broader shoulders, straighter backs

in economical relations, could be of any advantage to them.
would you like to hide in my wage packet cocoon?

By changes in the material conditions of existence,
you can touch the sides in my conjurer's cocoon

this form of Socialism, however, by no means understands
abolition of the bourgeois relations of production
*one where the solution for evolution is the ablution of revolution,
rather than*

an abolition that can be affected only by a revolution
in case you needed reminding

but administrative reforms, based on the continued existence of
these relations
*so let's clean the carpet and hope no-one can see the bumps
underneath*

reforms, therefore, that in no respect affect the relations between
capital and labour
*You say laughter and I say larfter, You say after and I say arfter,
Laughter, larfter, after, arfter, let's call the whole thing off*

but, at the best, lessen the cost, and simplify the administrative
work, of bourgeois government
here is where Taylor would swear a worker is studious in working
slowly to convince their boss they are working quickly

Bourgeois Socialism attains adequate expression when, and only
when, it becomes a mere figure of speech.
'Presentiment — is that long shadow — on the lawn — Indicative
that Suns go down — The notice to the startled Grass — That
Darkness — is about to pass —' (ED)

Free trade: for the benefit of the working class
the oxy, the moron, the pointedly foolish notion

Protective duties: for the benefit of the working class.
you want your country back? Okay, then let me know who took it

Prison Reform: for the benefit of the working class.
lock up the lords, lock up the earls, relieve all the ladies of all of
their pearls

This is the last word and the only seriously meant word of
bourgeois socialism.
there is a line across our cheeks, from sitting so long on the edge
of our seats

It is summed up in the phrase: the bourgeois is a bourgeois — for
the benefit of the working class
I don't want clever conversation, I never want to work that hard, I
just want someone who'll work for me, I want you just the way you
are (BJ)

3. Critical-Utopian Socialism and Communism

We do not here refer to that literature which, in every great modern revolution
that tried to wipe the windows clean without a damp chamois, and

has always given voice to the demands of the proletariat, such as the writings of Babeuf and others.
dear Gracchus, what did you say? Society must be made to operate in such a way that it eradicates once and for all the desire of a man to become richer, or wiser, or more powerful than others.

The first direct attempts of the proletariat to attain its own ends, made in times of universal excitement
the winds of change blew a cold breeze up bell bottom trousers making a shrivel of the rich

when feudal society was being overthrown, necessarily failed, owing to the then undeveloped state of the proletariat
look at the state of you, there's a revolution to be had here, clean yourself up, I'll meet you out the front – don't forget your hammer and sickle

as well as to the absence of the economic conditions for its emancipation
let's be clear, in order to be free, the price of everything, even our lives, must be beyond our reach

conditions that had yet to be produced, and could be produced by the impending bourgeois epoch alone
patience, as well as universal penury, is what is required, to let the bourgeoisie amass their end

The revolutionary literature that accompanied these first
movements of the proletariat had necessarily a reactionary
character.
Lord let us change the things we can, etc....

It inculcated universal asceticism and social levelling in its
crudest form.
*our age knows nothing but reaction, and leaps from one extreme
to another (RN)*

The Socialist and Communist systems, properly so called
by men, who live in the departments of well-meaning

those of Saint-Simon
*a meretricious advocate for working class utility, held back by
working class frivolity*

Fourier
*a co-operative fellow, seeking material abundance with
contributable reward*

Owen, and others
*who saw no battle between nature and nurture, for a co-operative
culture will determine our futures*

spring into existence in the early undeveloped period
*ahead of their time and not lost for words, they lost sleep putting
the clock forwards*

The founders of these systems see, indeed, the class antagonisms
they hide theirs under the bonnet, but sometimes it's in a hat

as well as the action of the decomposing elements in the
prevailing form of society.
*the stink, the stench, the stew, of land, of finery, of the grand who's
who*

[129]

But the proletariat, as yet in its infancy, offers to them the spectacle of a class
romper suit toddlers just out of bed, swinging the hammer but never the lead

without any historical initiative or any independent political movement.
what has gone on before, is a mere mixing of the mortar

Since the development of class antagonism keeps even pace with the development of industry
and such industry has a long way to go, for

the economic situation, as they find it, does not as yet offer to them the material conditions for the emancipation of the proletariat.
we have to let it run its course, the antibiotics of capitalism are losing all their force

They therefore search after a new social science, after new social laws, that are to create these conditions
they seek him here, they seek him there, up the chimney, under the stairs

Historical action is to yield to their personal inventive action;
what is this thing called history, the actions of people or those of theory

historically created conditions of emancipation to fantastic ones
reach for the stars, climb every mountain higher, reach for the stars, follow your heart's desire (SC7)

and the gradual, spontaneous class organisation of the proletariat to an organisation of society especially contrived by these inventors
I think we've solved it Watson. By jove I believe we have Holmes

Only from the point of view of being the most suffering class
does the proletariat exist for them
*they are the poor's camera obscura, shining the light of poverty on
the walls of the bourgeoisie*

Future history resolves itself, in their eyes
look into my eyes, not around my eyes, look into my eyes, 3,2,1,
you're under (LB)

into the propaganda and the practical carrying out of their social
plans.
'I have not been taking your panties home, putting them on
in my bedroom and then parading up and down in front of the
mirror...3,2,1, you're back in the room (LB)

In the formation of their plans
a surreal 19th century mixtape of injustice

they are conscious of caring chiefly for the interests of the
working class, as being the most suffering class
'blessed are the poor in spirit, for theirs is the kingdom of heaven'
(M 5:3)

Only from the point of view of being the most suffering class does
the proletariat exist for them
they are the poor's camera obscura, shining the light of poverty on
the walls of the bourgeoisie

The undeveloped state of the class struggle, as well as their own
surroundings
they can hop up and suckle a muckle of human kindness, but must
not run amok in the playground

causes Socialists of this kind to consider themselves far superior
to all class antagonisms
their palms were marked with sympathy, their brains were empty
of empathy

They want to improve the condition of every member of society,
even that of the most favoured
universal basic income for all, from which the rich will pay their
cleaners, but the poor can still buy fuck all

Hence, they habitually appeal to society at large, without the
distinction of class; nay, by preference, to the ruling class.
nay, nay and thrice nay, titter ye not, for these socialists felt they
could help the lot

For how can people, when once they understand their system
a picture round, fingers on buzzers, can you name this parliament
of buzzards?

fail to see in it the best possible plan of the best possible state of
society?
the beholder's eye does not see 'as neere is Fancie to Beautie, as
the pricke to the Rose, as the stalke to the rynde, as the earth to
the roote' (JL)

Hence, they reject all political, and especially all revolutionary
action
for them a crossed sword is a crossed word

they wish to attain their ends by peaceful means, necessarily
doomed to failure,
The tigers of wrath are wiser than the horses of instruction (WB)

and by the force of example, to pave the way for the new social
Gospel
all praise the Gospel of a world already broken, a spell seen by
Marx as a failed token

Such fantastic pictures of future society
some of which can be seen from space, by a select group shot
there by Elon Musk

painted at a time when the proletariat is still in a very
undeveloped state
beaten down like molten metal, then plunged into water to be set
for time

and has but a fantastic conception of its own position
I'm Spartacus, no I'm Spartacus, no, it's my turn, you were
sacrificed last time

correspond with the first instinctive yearnings of that class for a
general reconstruction of society.
a monumental change at the flick of a wrist, blink once and they'll
have had your chips

But these Socialist and Communist publications contain also a
critical element.
one that it is more than a testament, for

They attack every principle of existing society.
one that has roots in Hegelian sobriety

Hence, they are full of the most valuable materials
a light soufflé of something ethereal

for the enlightenment of the working class.
to give them a test they hope they can pass

The practical measures proposed in them —
please refer to footnote 10, in Chapter 9, Section 8, sub-section 7,
bullet point 6, 5, 4, 3, 2, 1...fire!

such as the abolition of the distinction between town and country
something of this has taken place, there's more people in town now
with a country face

of the family
who up to now have been factory fodder

of the carrying on of industries for the account of private
individuals
we know all about wallets that fly away to far offshores

and of the wage system
that belittles the little that zeros earn

the proclamation of social harmony
I hereby announce happiness like gold, is to be measured by the
ounce

the conversion of the function of the state into a more
superintendence of production —
ello, ello, ello, what do we have here then, a parlous state indeed

all these proposals point solely to the disappearance of class
antagonisms
fair or fowl, fight or flight, this is what life's all about (NB: read in
a Northern Irish accent if you want it to rhyme)

which were, at that time, only just cropping up
the daffodils are early this year, but I fear a Spring frost

and which, in these publications, are recognised in their earliest
indistinct and undefined forms only
there's a drawing board over there, now get back to it

These proposals, therefore, are of a purely Utopian character
the proof is in these puddings, who are full of dough that will not
rise

The significance of Critical-Utopian Socialism and Communism
bears an inverse relation to historical development
the builder who has come to give us a quote, sucks his teeth in
despair, they slip down his throat

In proportion as the modern class struggle develops and takes
definite shape
as it did, in various dimensions, various disguises, various speeds

this fantastic standing apart from the contest, these fantastic
attacks on it
from the side-lines of theory

lose all practical value and all theoretical justification
dirty hands and a clear mind, were not their way, I think you'll find

Therefore, although the originators of these systems were, in
many respects, revolutionary
in formulating a change to the hierarchical norm,

their disciples have, in every case, formed mere reactionary sects
that cosset and covet for mere microbrial change

They hold fast by the original views of their masters
students should never accept all that they learn

in opposition to the progressive historical development of the
proletariat
see: Moore's Law of time, for a doubling of change

They, therefore, endeavour, and that consistently, to deaden the
class struggle and to reconcile the class antagonisms.
'make up, make up, never ever break up, if you do you'll catch the
flu, and that will be the end of you'

They still dream of experimental realisation of their social Utopias
schemers and dreamers, testing testing, are you believers?

of founding isolated 'phalansteres',
there is a streak of anti-semitism in Fourier's furrowing here

of establishing "Home Colonies"
an idea of Owen's, with a mixture in housing to leave nobody owing

or setting up a "Little Icaria" — duodecimo editions of the New Jerusalem
a movement of Cabet's to some American States, where egalité turned to factional debate

and to realise all these castles in the air they are compelled to appeal to the feelings and purses of the bourgeois
when money doesn't hang from trees, you must always go to the source of the greed

By degrees, they sink into the category of the reactionary [or] conservative Socialists
man, what a con, to be in love with such oxymorons

depicted above, differing from these only by more systematic pedantry
and there is nothing more systematic than pedantry

and by their fanatical and superstitious belief in the miraculous effects of their social science
abracadabra, bish bash bosh, we've made a Utopia out of ological tosh

They, therefore, violently oppose all political action on the part of the working class
I'm not really sure if that is true, but when Marx is on a roll, then what can you do?

such action, according to them, can only result from blind unbelief in the new Gospel
do as we say, and do as we do, and life will be better for you and for you

The Owenites in England, and the Fourierists in France, respectively, oppose the Chartists and the Réformistes.
Engels thought highly of Owen though, writing articles for his New Moral World, and Owen was President of the first TUC, but as for Fourier? C'est la vie!

'Another world is not only possible, she is on her way, and if you listen carefully, you can hear her breathing'
(Arundhati Roy)

Part Four

Position of the Communists in Relation to the Various Existing Opposition Parties

Part Four: Position Of The Communists in Relation to the Various Existing Opposition Parties

(aka, musical chairs that sing as well as dance — maestro? Begin!)

The Communists fight for the attainment of the immediate aims
what do we want? [insert want]

for the enforcement of the momentary interests of the working class;
when do we want it? [when class antagonisms reach their peak?]
because when you are only halfway up, you are neither up nor down

but in the movement of the present, they also represent and take care of the future of that movement
'for when there's no future, how can there be sin, we are the flowers in the dustbin' (SP)

In France, the Communists ally with the Social-Democrats
avec Ledru-Rollin, Louis Blanc, et Reformé, le parfum du socialisme

against the conservative and radical bourgeoisie, reserving, however
they are forever covered in reservations

the right to take up a critical position in regard to phases and illusions traditionally handed down from the great Revolution.
they have drawn red, white and blue lines in the sand

In Switzerland, they support the Radicals, without losing sight of the fact that this party consists of antagonistic elements
always with the antagonisms, can we not just get on with it already?

partly of Democratic Socialists, in the French sense, partly of
radical bourgeois
a bit like a paint mix from Farrow & Ball, far from the low jinx of
Cannon & Ball

In Poland, they support the party that insists on an agrarian
revolution as the prime condition for national emancipation,
the lie of the land, will always form the foundation, whether fallow
or not

that party which fomented the insurrection of Cracow in 1846
where a Berlin-like scene of division was the result of 1815

In Germany, they fight with the bourgeoisie whenever it acts in a
revolutionary way
hey Johnny, what are you rebelling against? What've you got?
(TWO)

against the absolute monarchy, the feudal squirearchy, and the
petty bourgeoisie
'well, today, we have a melange of absolute petty feudal noodles'.
'Yum, yum'

But they never cease, for a single instant, to instil into the working
class
that mental fight, so their swords never sleep in their hands (WB,
kind of)

the clearest possible recognition of the hostile antagonism
between bourgeoisie and proletariat
as if they need telling, with the ever-present clash of pestilence and
pomp

in order that the German workers may straightway use
ready-made revolt in rich-proof gloves

as so many weapons against the bourgeoisie
who are your enemies' enemy, and thus your foe

the social and political conditions that the bourgeoisie must
necessarily introduce along with its supremacy
that gust of new-born wind sweeping across Europe with the
effectiveness of a G4S prison guard

and in order that, after the fall of the reactionary classes
in Germany, the fight against the bourgeoisie itself may
immediately begin
so lace up your toughest conkers and let battle commence

The Communists turn their attention chiefly to Germany
it's been as good a place as any since then

because that country is on the eve of a bourgeois revolution
'But you tell me over and over and over again my friend, Ah, you
don't believe we're on the eve of destruction' (PFS)

that is bound to be carried out under more advanced conditions
of European civilisation
Ich bin am zivilisiertesten — Non, Je suis le plus civilisé — Us
Brits have never been civilised

and with a much more developed proletariat than that of
England was in the seventeenth
and that was the most revolutionary us Brits ever got, strikes and
riots are now our lot

and France in the eighteenth century
yet, looking back, as revolutions go, that was top of the stack

and because the bourgeois revolution in Germany will be but the
prelude to an immediately following proletarian revolution
fingers crossed, legs crossed, arms crossed, eyes crossed, you spin

[145]

me right round baby, right round

In short, the Communists everywhere support every revolutionary movement against the existing social and political order of things
so we will fight them on the beaches, build our own sandcastles in the air out of their reach

In all these movements, they bring to the front, as the leading question in each the property question
still a play for the day, not who owns the construction, but who owns the means of production

no matter what its degree of development at the time
I'm late, I'm late for a very important state

Finally, they labour everywhere for the union and agreement of the democratic parties of all countries
Lift up our glasses and watch your palaces burn to ashes, Fucking fascists, who the fuck are you to give fifty lashes (RTJ)

The Communists disdain to conceal their views and aims
Coming, ready or not!

They openly declare that their ends can be attained only by the forcible overthrow of all existing social conditions.
I hereby declare this revolution open for business - may Marx approve it, and all who sail in it

Let the ruling classes tremble at a Communistic revolution
Let's get ready to rumble, watch us wreck the mike, watch us wreck the mike, watch us wreck the mike, psyche! (A&D)

The proletarians have nothing to lose but their chains
& high-vis jackets, tabards, uniforms, see through knickers & a peephole bra, plus endless hours away from those near & dear
They have a world to win

'Another world is not only possible, she is on her way, and if you listen carefully, you can hear her breathing' (AR).

Working Men of All Countries, Unite!
women too & all those from below, at the back, and in between —
peace out!

Images

Front Cover image: Samuel Raynard

Part One
(Creative Commons images in order of their appearance)

Chained Prometheus — by Jacques de l'Ange (circa 1640–1650)

Plebeians — Article, 'Plebeians Address and Patricians Response' (source: https://bit.ly/2uUofIN)

The Baker and I — by Neil Moralee (source: https://bit.ly/2Hee6sW)

Royal Wedding in Mother — by Anne (source: https://bit.ly/2H9taup)

Fixed Fee — by eltpics (source: https://bit.ly/2Jr9r7A)

People work on computers at the Busy Internet computer center in Accra — World Bank Photo Library (source: https://bit.ly/2qekWr7)

Three Witches Glamis Castle Macbeth Trail (source: https://www.glamis—castle.co.uk/the—castle/the—gardens/the—macbeth—trail/)

Fight the Power — by Harnelle Hailey (source: https://bit.ly/2ICs33i)

Gold Lamborghini Veneno Roadster (source: any posh car dealer)

Belmati Jonko, India — The National (souce: https://www.thenational.ae/opinion/in—india—the—division—is—simple—rich—or—poor—1.116655)

Newspaper Club — by Nada News Pepe Medina (source: https://bit.ly/2Eut6Qn)

Workers — by sean 808080 (source: https://bit.ly/2GH6H4d)

Ties that Bind Hands — by Publicity Pod (source: https://bit.ly/2JtNzIB)

Empire — by Wolfgang (source: https://bit.ly/2IDzIyv)

Groundhog — by Pascal (source: https://bit.ly/2JtNtkp)

Hot Air Balloon — by Eric BC Lim (source: https://bit.ly/2qgQegh)

Part Two

Freedom — by Antonio Acuna (source: https://bit.ly/2GKNvGL)

Berlin Graffiti — by The Naked Ape (source: https://bit.ly/2GH1kCc)

Private Property No Trespassing — by BXGD (source: https://bit.ly/2qbLZ6s)

The Two Ronnies with John Cleese — BBC

Royal Caribbean Grandeur of the Seas cruise ship casino roulette — by C Watts (source: https://bit.ly/2uW7j4D)

Dogs Gambling in Sand — by Javier Candeira (source: https://bit.ly/2HinXxV)

David Cameron 2010 The Year for Change? — by Mongo (source: https://bit.ly/2JvmCEC)

Meat Grinder — by Gage Skidmore (source: https://bit. ly/2JrKusG)

Chile Education Rally/Violent Protest — by C64—92 (source: https://bit.ly/2qbivWf)

Ideas are Immune to Tear Gas — by Teacher Dude (source: https://bit.ly/2qfasrg)

Commandments — by In Da Mist (source: https://bit. ly/2ICCQuf)

Buenos Aires: Parc Patricios — by Wally Gobetz (source: https:// bit.ly/2qePTLP)

The Revolution — by Elvert Barnes (source: https://bit. ly/2GQ6pYX)

19th Century Read the Riot Act Poster — by University of Reading (source: https://bit.ly/2JB4IQI)

Part Three

Evolution of the Hipster — by insta: @ablekay47 (source: https:// bit.ly/2HeqoFq)

Buckeye Valley Food Bank — by Kevin Dooley (source: https:// bit.ly/2GPvGT7)

Non-violence — by the United Nations (source: https://bit. ly/2qiOrqS)

Death — by Andrea Kirby (source: https://bit.ly/2HcrYGh)

Democracy — by Filippo Minelli (source: https://bit.ly/2v8zxJy)

Anarchy Cupcake — by Stephanie (source: https://bit.ly/2EAT1G2)

Photography and the Law — by Rohan Kar (source: https://bit.ly/2uZAS5j)

Poverty — by Harry Kaufmann (source: https://bit.ly/2IGpMUI)

Danbo, his name — by Tim Li (source: https://bit.ly/2v4wDoX)

Amazon Forest — by Oregon State University (source: https://bit.ly/2IKib7t)

Part Four

Black Lives Matter — by 5chw4r7z (source: https://bit.ly/2EylYCp)

Wealth — by Richie Diesterheft (source: https://bit.ly/2EBk9od)